John S. Black

The Christian Consciousness

Its relation to evolution in morals and in doctrine

John S. Black

The Christian Consciousness
Its relation to evolution in morals and in doctrine

ISBN/EAN: 9783337262617

Printed in Europe, USA, Canada, Australia, Japan

Cover: Foto ©Lupo / pixelio.de

More available books at **www.hansebooks.com**

THE

CHRISTIAN CONSCIOUSNESS

Its Relation to Evolution

IN MORALS AND IN DOCTRINE

BY

J. S. BLACK

BOSTON
LEE AND SHEPARD PUBLISHERS
10 MILK STREET
1895

TYPOGRAPHY BY C. J. PETERS & SON, BOSTON.
PRESSWORK BY S. J. PARKHILL & CO.

PREFACE

The literature that has been devoted to the "Christian Consciousness" has been of a fragmentary character. It has been employed for special purposes from the time of Schleiermacher to the present day. This will appear more at length in the course of this work. But the employment of any tenet in philosophy or in doctrine for special purposes, while it demonstrates the apologetic value of the doctrine, is unfavorable to its general reception and systematic study. It receives little more than a passing notice from writers on systematic theology and dogma. It has been called into the court of public discussion as a witness in favor of sensationalism, of Andover theology so-called, and of various views in eschatology. The opponents of these views naturally and almost inevitably regarded the witness with suspicion. Current controversy partakes largely of the nature of special pleading, and the first thing to do was to discredit the character and the testimony of the witness.

There are several questions that must be answered, such as: What is consciousness? Is there a Christian consciousness? If there is, what are its relations to consciousness in general, and to the religious consciousness in particular? What are its functions? Has it been hitherto neglected? Is it an old and well-known phase of the truth masquerading under a new name, or is it a hitherto much neglected and little used part of the armor of the Christian apologist?

In an interview with General Booth, he is reported to have said that, while he believed the Bible and wished men to read it, the aim of his army was to bring men to God rather than to the Book. Their endeavor was to get men to pray. This was the point of contact with God. He admitted that he rather dreaded Bible classes, because they got men into disputation. Removed from the Salvation Army by a whole diameter, but moving in the same circle, we find the German theologians, to whom the usually accepted proofs of the inspiration of Scripture are unsatisfactory and insufficient, but who can accept their inspiration by the appeal to, and the testimony of, the Christian consciousness. Less logical and more vague, but of equal significance, is the Christo-centric contemporary theology.

The study of the Christian consciousness is in its infancy, but the study of it is an aid to the development of it. It seems strange, at this end of the nineteenth century of the Christian era, that there should be an undeveloped, and partly unused, function of the Christian life; a function which not only accounts for moral and dogmatic phenomena, but also makes God more real to men. It comes at a time of need. The glory of the Reformation was the exaltation of faith, and the substituting the infallible Bible for the infallible church. But when infallible systems of theology took the place of the infallible book, the church, that had glowed in its contact with the living Word, became chilled at the touch of dead orthodoxies. The exaltation of the Word became a delusion and a snare when pains and penalties were attached to any interpretation of it differing from that of the majority. The immediate result of the Reformation was the formulation of several creeds and orders of church government, each of which made a practical claim of infallibility for its own faith and discipline. In days of polemic warfare the scent for heresy becomes keener and keener. It was in order to reason and debate concerning the letter of the Word, but it was dangerous to speak too freely about its spirit. If any one was rash enough to appeal to his own inner light, his own Christian consciousness and divine persuasion, it was at once declared to be a presumption and spiritual pride that savored of blasphemy. The tyranny of creeds resembles political tyrannies in its instinctive desire to keep men under. The dismal exaltation of the divine sovereignty until it distorted the character of God was the instinctive though undesigned policy of ecclesiastical oligarchies. The Christian consciousness had to hide its diminished head, and even doubt and condemn itself. Times have changed, and the Christian consciousness has its part to play in the momentous era of change and development on which the world seems to be entering. Hitherto we have spoken of the Bible, the church, and the reason as being sources of authority. To these three the spirit of the age demands the addition of the Christian consciousness, as being not only a source of authority in and of itself, but also as being a touchstone for the trying of the Bible, the church, and the reason.

CONTENTS

CHAPTER I

THE CHRISTIAN CONSCIOUSNESS

What is it? — Theories about consciousness supplementary to, rather than antagonistic to, each other. — Locke, Cousin, Descartes, Sir William Hamilton, McCosh, Kant, Herbert Spencer. — Instinct, intuition, consciousness. — Religious and Christian consciousness. Opinions of Dean Mansell, William F. Warren, D.D., Professor Candlish, Professor Kaftan. — Definition of the Christian consciousness. — Its imperative categories. — Illumination that comes from willing to do God's will. — Reformation theology not favorable to the doctrine of the Christian consciousness. — Contemporary misconceptions as to Christian consciousness. — Relation of the Christian consciousness to progressive morality 1

CHAPTER II

THE DIGNITY OF MAN

Reformation theology belittled man. — It was one-sided. — Lecky on exaggerations of human depravity. — The Eighth Psalm. — Elohim. — Christian consciousness sees both sides of this truth. — Evolution testifies to the dignity of man. — Professor Drummond's "Ascent of Man." — Obscurity of the beginnings of all civilization. — The progress of English-speaking peoples. — Italy. — England. — Scotland. — United States. — Sir William Dawson on inspired achievement 26

CHAPTER III

THE DESTINY OF MAN

The qualifications of the infallibility of the Scriptures. — Infallibility not claimed for the Christian consciousness. — The honor it puts upon man. — Evolution and man. — Future possibilities for him do not meet the Scriptural statements concerning him. — His destiny a future of divine possibilities. — Three great missing links. — Mr. Huxley's view of development coming to an end. — The estimate which science makes of man. — The Christian consciousness accepts and approves his dignity and destiny 46

CHAPTER IV

THE EVOLUTION OF MORALS

Considerations that have prejudiced certain thinkers against Christian consciousness. — Schleiermacher. — The Ritchslian school. — Professor Harris. — Dr. Francis Patton. — Dr. Behrends. — Standards of Scripture interpretation. — Herbert Spencer. — Henry Lewes. — Historians of civilization. — Utilitarianism. — The struggle for existence. — Present-day sociology. — Maurice's social morality, theoretical and practical. — Views of Benjamin Kidd and Professor Drummond 61

CHAPTER V

THE CHRISTIAN CONSCIOUSNESS AND SLAVERY

In ancient times. — In Puritan times. — John Bacon's will. — The evolution of opinion about slavery. — The relation of discovery and invention to evolution in morals. — The earlier opponents of slavery. — Samuel Sewall. — Legal action of different countries. — Opinions of Washington, Jefferson, Monroe, and Patrick Henry.— Opinions of clergymen during the War of the Rebellion. — The political economist's explanation. — Dr. Munger on slavery. — The part played by the Christian consciousness . . .   82

CHAPTER VI

THE CHRISTIAN CONSCIOUSNESS AS RELATED TO INTEMPERANCE, THE OPIUM TRADE, AND GAMBLING

Total abstinence a recent reform. — The former and present relation of the church to it. — The Abstemii. — The Nazarites. — Parallel between slavery and intemperance. — Opium trade. — Its unique character. — The conscience of Britain against it. — The secret of its power. — Relation of enlightened public sentiment to the Christian consciousness. — Gambling the vice common to heathenism and to Christianity. — The possibility of heathenism condemning gambling. — The growth of Christian sentiment against gambling. — Mercantile gambling. — Huxley's pessimism. — Silence of Scripture on this vice. — Professor Proctor. — Similar questions that might be considered 103

CHAPTER VII

THE ATTITUDE OF THE CHURCH TO EVOLUTION IN MORALS

The charges brought against the church, and the inferences therefrom. — Misrepresentation of the church. — Its human side. — Its size. — Its age. — Its prime function. — Its lax discipline in regard to conduct, and its vigilance in dogma. — The environment of moral movements. — The union with the state. — The opposite extreme. — The church not a club 125

CHAPTER VIII

THE CHRISTIAN CONSCIOUSNESS, AND THE RELIGIOUS CONSCIOUSNESS OF THE HEATHEN WORLD

Agreement of geology and revelation. — Sir William Dawson's view. — Noah. — Abraham. — Melchisedec. — Job. — Jethro, Baalam. — Contact of Hebrew and Greek. — Septuagint. — Huxley. — The logos. — The condition of the religious consciousness when Christ came. — The centuries of silence. — Greek thought. — Buddhism. — Confucianism and Taoism. — The condition of morality when Jesus was on earth . 142

CHAPTER IX

THE RELATION OF THE CHRISTIAN CONSCIOUSNESS TO DOCTRINE

Has there been an evolution of doctrine? — The difficulty of separating morals from doctrine. — Various definitions of doctrine. — The salvation of infants. — Original sin and inherited guilt. — Sacramentarianism. — The spirit of the age. — Salvation of the heathen. — Andover theology. — Rational sanctions and exegetical justification. — Do Christians believe that the heathen are perishing? — Features common to infant salvation, and the salvation of the heathen. — The character of God, when involved. — The legal infliction of torture. — Exceptions to the prevailing belief. — What has brought about the change? 163

CHAPTER X

CHRISTIAN CONSCIOUSNESS AND WOMAN'S PLACE IN THE CHURCH

A question of doctrine as well as of polity. — Paul's teaching. — Woman's place in the Roman Catholic Church. — Opinion of Robinson of Leyden. — Woman's evolution as a teacher. — As a Christian worker. — Study of medicine. —

Salvation Army. — Young People's Society of Christian Endeavor. — Woman in college and in theological seminaries. — Application to this question of Mr. Kidd's philosophy. — Of Professor Drummond's. — George MacDonald's view. — The "Gesta Christi." — Woman in the religious community. — In the age of chivalry 183

CHAPTER XI

CHRISTIAN CONSCIOUSNESS AND THE SIXTH COMMANDMENT

The thirst for blood. — War. — The War of the Rebellion. — A moral problem. — As a peacemaker Christianity has been a failure. — The duel. — Severities of the criminal code. — Judicial combat. — The prize-ring and college football. — Danger a popular attraction. — Societies for the prevention of cruelty to animals. — Admiration of personal daring. — Danger of the loss of manliness and courage. — The moral force of Charles Loring Brace. — The problem presented in this chapter 202

CHAPTER XII

OBJECTIONS AND POSSIBILITIES

Objections to evolution in morals. — View of President E. G. Robinson. — Unchanging morality. — When true. — Non-Christian ethical systems. — The divine and the human thought. — Joseph Cook. — Christian consciousness and sectarianism. — Hindrance to union. — Schleiermacher's views. — Eschatology. — The questions raised by physical science and by the higher criticism not to be dreaded. — The moral difficulties are real and persistent. — Various kinds of doubt. — The revealing of the Father. — The eve of great changes. — Young Men's Christian Associations, The Salvation Army, and Young People's Society of Christian Endeavor. — The healing of schism 219

THE CHRISTIAN CONSCIOUSNESS

CHAPTER I

THE CHRISTIAN CONSCIOUSNESS

Consciousness is the knowledge of that which passes in one's own mind. It is at once the knowledge and the power to know. It is the instrument of observation as well as of introspection; and therefore by the observations of consciousness we can attain to conclusions as to principles or morals before we have had experience to guide us. Physiology cannot furnish any explanation of thought or of consciousness. In common speech the knowledge of sensation is familiarly and vaguely expressed by this word, and we have modifying phrases which are not always philosophically accurate. Such expressions as partially conscious, painfully conscious, semi-conscious, and fully conscious, may not be exact terms in metaphysics, but they convey ideas with sufficient clearness.

What is consciousness? What is the province of it? and what is the power of it? are questions which have been keenly debated by the various schools of philosophy. Is the pure development of reason better secured by abstraction from all finite and material objects, than by mingling with and comprehending the world in which we live? This question was old in the days of Aristotle. Know thyself is the watchword of philosophy. Knowledge of one's self is consciousness, but not the whole of consciousness. It has been well said that the possibility of science and of morality rests on the universality of consciousness. Man comes out of a past about which he learns more or less; and he dies at the threshold of a future concerning which reason has taught him to anticipate a little, and faith has enabled him to prophesy many things. He is a limited fragment of an unknown whole; but he can look over the edge of his territory into the undiscovered country, for he can reason from particulars to generals. The unlimited and unexplored becomes a part of his consciousness. "It is by the God within that we can understand the God without." The Bible assures man that the things he does not know now he shall know hereafter; and this hereafter is not always and necessarily a future state of existence. Science declares that what he does not know now he may know hereafter. We live on an island called Earth. We are conscious of ourselves and of our surroundings; but we know only in part, for we have not yet explored the whole of our island. We are not yet masters of the world within or of the world without. The telescope and the spectroscope enable us to land some of the driftwood that floats to us from the other islands, called worlds, in this infinite sea; and we refuse to believe that this is all that we are to have, and all that we are to know. The story of the past echoes our heart-cry for more light. It tells of secret after secret unfolded. Subjective knowledge has not made as much progress as has objective knowledge.

The theories about, and the definitions of, consciousness that have been advanced by moralists and metaphysicians, may be regarded as being not antagonistic to each other, but rather as supplementary to each other. Locke says that complex ideas can be resolved into simple ideas; and that simple ideas come to us through sense perception; that is, by the gateway of the physical senses. This is sensation. The second factor to the production of an idea is reflection. But reflection is another name for consciousness. In many things Locke is more orthodox than he knew himself to be, or than he intended to be. He exalts sense perception, but he has done good in calling attention to the relation of the physical senses to ideas. Cousin says, "Consciousness is composed of three inseparable elements; viz., sensibility, or sense perception; activity, or liberty; and reason. The middle element, activity or liberty, is a sort of postulate between sensibility and reason." The sensibility and reason of Cousin are the sensation and reflection of Locke. Descartes' famous "*Cogito, ergo sum*" is the reason of Cousin and the reflection of Locke. The primary data of consciousness, according to Sir William Hamilton, are truths of perception and truths of reason. He is a realist, and exalts the dictates of consciousness. We do not, however, assert that idealists belittle the commanding power of consciousness. In the words of McCosh, "We know self as having being, existence. The knowledge we have in self-consciousness, which is associated with every intelligent act, is not an impression, as Hume would say, nor a mere quality or attribute, as certain of the Scottish metaphysicians affirm, nor a phenomenon in the sense of appearance, as Kant supposes, but of a thing or reality." Kant affirms that space and time are the forms given by the mind to the phenomena which are presented through the senses, and are not to be supposed as having anything more than a subjective existence. McCosh holds this to be a fatal heresy, and opposed to the revelations of consciousness. In his well-known chapter on the "Physiology of Laughter," Herbert Spencer says, "There is still another direction in which any excited portion of the nervous system may discharge itself: and a direction in which it usually does discharge itself when the excitement is not strong. It may pass on the stimulus to some other portion of the nervous system. This is what occurs in quiet thinking and feeling. The successive states which constitute consciousness result from this. . . . While we are totally unable to comprehend how the excitement of certain nerves should generate feeling, — while, in the production of consciousness by physical agents acting on physical structure, we come to an absolute mystery, never to be solved, it is yet quite possible for us to know by observation what are the successive forms which this absolute mystery may take." This is materialism pure and simple.

A certain amount of confusion arises from permitting ourselves to get into a habit of indefinite thinking about instinct, intuition, and consciousness. An instinct is a faculty independent of instruction and prior to experience. When we use such expressions as "instinctive reverence," "instinctive worship," our words are meaningless, except in so far as they are misleading. The errors of the pulpit in the use of the words instinct and instinctive are many and various. An intuition is a self-evident, necessary, and universal truth. It is not mere insight, nor is it illumination, whether sacred or secular. It is not inspiration, which is the gift of infallibility in proclaiming moral and religious truth. It is not illumination, which is the glow and white heat with which light comes to our minds. Inspiration may produce this intellectual glow; but it may and usually does come as the result of ratiocination, or of memory, or of unconscious cerebration and association of ideas. The intuitions of the mind are not before consciousness, nor are they identical with consciousness, or parallel with it, but rather should we say that our intuitions are supplied by the exercise of consciousness and memory. We have the fruits and results of metaphysics, but the question is as to origin rather than as to mode. It is not *a priori* or *a posteriori*, realist or idealist, deductive or inductive: for to-day the query is is not, What is consciousness? but, Whence is it? Is our conception materialistic or theistic?

Sir William Hamilton declares that "no difficulty emerges in theology which had not previously emerged in philosophy." It is impossible to conceive of the Christian or religious consciousness which is not of theistic origin.[1]

---

[1] Many writers, while not expressing themselves very definitely, seem to imply that the religious consciousness is quite possible in any form of belief. Livingstone in his last journal remarks that he never had met with an African chief whom he could not make ashamed of selling his own people into slavery, but arousing the conscience is not the creating of religious consciousness. It must always be a question as to how near the theistic conception the more thoughtful heathen are, while within the borders of civilization we may grant the personal honesty of non-theists, who may call themselves agnostics,

In the use of the terms "Christian Consciousness" and "religious consciousness" as interchangeable, it is to be borne in mind that while practically no confusion of thought results, the terms are not synonymous. All Christian consciousness is religious consciousness; but all religious consciousness is not, therefore, Christian consciousness. The Buddhist and Mohammedan have a religious consciousness which is not Christian. The Christian consciousness differs from theirs not only in degree, but also in kind. What is Christian consciousness? This question has had many answers. Dean Mansell, in his Bampton Lectures entitled the "Limits of Religious Thought," reasons from the general conditions of all human consciousness that there is a necessary limitation to its powers, and therefore an inability to conceive the Infinite. His conditions of consciousness are: —

(1) Distinction between one object and another.

(2) Relation between subject and object.

or materialists, or atheists, and yet refuse to believe in the possibility of their being able to free themselves from the theistic conception.

(3) Succession and duration in time.

(4) Personality.

He holds that the religious consciousness is reflective and intuitive. The reasonings of the reflective consciousness are sufficient to correct our conception of a supreme being, but not sufficient to originate such a conception. The other part of consciousness — religious intuition — manifests itself in the feeling of dependence, and in the conviction of moral obligation. These two conditions beget prayer and expiation. Dependence implies a personal superior, hence our conviction of the power of God. Moral obligation implies a moral lawgiver, hence our conviction of the goodness of God. His limits of religious consciousness are: —

(1) That a sense of dependence is not a consciousness of the absolute and the infinite.

(2) Nor is a sense of moral obligation a consciousness of the absolute and the infinite.

(3) Religious consciousness implies the infinite.

(4) God is known as a person through the consciousness of ourselves as persons. There can be no philosophical theism without this

consciousness. The materialist or the pantheist who denies his own personality is on the straight road to atheism.

Fifteen years after Dean Mansell's book was published, the Rev. William F. Warren, D.D., Dean of the Boston University School of Theology, delivered one of the Boston lectures on "Christianity and Scepticism." His theme was "The Christian Consciousness: its apologetic value." His position is: —

(1) Every man has some sort of religious consciousness, e.g., theistic, pantheistic, polytheistic, atheistic.

There are sub-types of religious consciousness, e.g., Jewish, Christian, Mohammedan.

His leading traits of the ideal Christian consciousness are: —

(1) An immediate knowledge or feeling or realization of some kind of personal communion with God. He subdivides into the Old Testament religions or God-consciousness, the ordinary Christian consciousness, and the higher-life Christian consciousness. The apologetic value of the Christian consciousness over the atheistic, polytheistic, and pantheistic is, that the votaries of these last three believe, but

the Christian knows. He holds that in the narrower field of controversy, where theistic naturalism and supranaturalism grapple, the facts of normal Christian consciousness forever settle, for its possessor, every speculative doubt and difficulty — that miracles and incarnation are easily grasped by Christian consciousness.

Professor Candlish, of the Free Church College, Glasgow, wrote the article "Dogmatic" in the ninth edition of the "Encyclopædia Britannica," since published in fuller shape in book form. He says, "The inward spiritual enlightenment of the believer corresponds very nearly to what has been called Christian consciousness." He ascribes the phrase to Schleiermacher, whose fundamental principle was that religion consists properly in feeling, and that we have an immediate consciousness of the divine — a God-consciousness. This Mansell denies. It will be found that the truth lies between the sensationalism of Schleiermacher and the intellectualism against which he revolted; but the difficulty is to find a meeting-place for sensationalism and intellectualism which will be satisfactory to both.

Professor Kaftan divides with Professor Harnack the honors of brilliance and popularity in the University of Berlin. He brings enthusiasm and spirituality to his work. He is the most distinguished advocate of the Ritschlian school of theology, the avowed object of which is to reconcile supranaturalism and rationalism. The task which this school has assigned itself does not seem as difficult of accomplishment as it did twenty years ago. With Schleiermacher they assert that the religious consciousness is the fountain of belief. They antagonize metaphysical statement of doctrine, and exalt the moral side of life and religion. While they maintain that the Holy Scriptures are the final and supreme authority in doctrine, because in them we have the Christian consciousness in its primitive purity, they are not orthodox on the question of inspiration.

This most popular school of religious thought in Germany of to-day has many attractive features; and it is certain, in the near future, to exercise wide influence in America. Religious consciousness as taught in Germany to-day exalts the subjective determination of truth, and in this lies its danger. The counterfeits of Christian consciousness will prove as dangerous as the exaggerations of it, or the ignoring of it. Like every real thing, it has to be sifted and tried, for it cannot be ignored.

Religious consciousness is consciousness plus the theistic conception; and Christian consciousness is religious consciousness with certain notable additions. These are: —

(1) What we know of our faith and of our feelings in the light of the revealed Word.

(2) What we know of our will to do God's will.

(3) What we know of the promised result of this willing to do God's will.

(4) What we know of being led by the Holy Spirit into truth.

(5) What we know of the witness of the Holy Spirit with our spirits as to our divine sonship.

The Holy Scriptures are the supreme authority in doctrine and in life. We do not claim, like the German school to which reference has been made, that the Holy Scriptures are in a sense subordinate to the Christian consciousness; nor need we, like Professor Candlish, maintain that the Christian consciousness is a subordinate authority. It is a co-ordinate authority. It is the illumined Word. It is not a primary and independent source of authority, but it takes the initiative in all change. Through it the new light from the Word of God flashes forth. We do not assert that the Christian consciousness is necessarily and always unerring.

The Papal claim of infallibility is not based on the Christian consciousness. There is no question as to the possibility of the Christian consciousness outgrowing the Holy Scriptures. It is as reasonable to speak of outgrowing the multiplication table as of outgrowing the Decalogue and the Sermon on the Mount. We make mistakes in our interpretation of the Scriptures. We make mistakes in our interpretation of the Christian consciousness. A mistake in dogma is an error; persistent error becomes the sin of heresy. A mistake of a moral kind is also an error. But the error of to-day often becomes the sin of the future.

God is immanent in mind and in matter. Man has a conscience. In that conscience, by God's immanence in mind, a moral law is revealed. A moral law leads naturally to the law-maker, the law-keeper, and the law-breaker.

The Word of God reveals the law-maker and the moral law. God's manifestation of himself in Christ illumines the sacred Word. Consciousness becomes Christian consciousness. It proves all things, and holds fast to that which is good. It has certain imperative categories which are its touchstones.

(1) What does the Word of God say?

(2) Is this or is it not the letter that kills?

(3) What is the spirit of it?

(4) In what way can moral certitude be attained?

(5) That is — How shall I know that the Spirit of truth is witnessing with my spirit?

(6) Shall not this be brought to the test of reason?

(7) Shall not the final appeal be the Christian consciousness?

It is self-evident that we cannot get from the Word of God that which is not in it; but there are treasures in it, both new and old. Our Lord tells us to search the Scriptures. The man who imagines that his Christian consciousness is to be the result of a miracle of grace, without effort on his part, is on the high road to fanaticism. " He that wills to do God's will shall know the doctrine." [1] Obedience to the divine will brings certitude to the soul with regard to moral truth. A single-hearted desire to please God illumines every question of a religious nature. Looked at from the standpoint of human philosophy, this is a most astounding assertion that Christ makes. When he uttered those words, earth listened to a new truth. He does not say, "If any man wills to do his will, he shall know that the teaching is wise or good or of superior excellence." Such statements as these are made every day. When any law or business scheme or system of government is presented to the individual or to the community, we examine it in the light of past experience, and of recognized laws and general principles, and come to a conclusion as to whether we should accept or reject this thing. Sometimes the result proves that we make a mistake. We are overpersuaded by the ingenious advocacy, or promoters and adopters of this new departure were equally mistaken.

When there is great conflict of opinion as to the advantage of this new thing, the plea usually is to give it a fair and practical trial.

[1] John vii. 17.

and by so doing demonstrate on which side the sound reasoning is. The political economy of our own and other countries is a practical illustration of this law in its working. That our putting the Scripture code into practice should convince us that it is very excellent, and suited to mankind, need excite no surprise. From the standpoint of secular history, Mosaic law is as worthy of study as is Roman or Greek law. One of the wonders of history is, that while Rome was in the zenith of her glory, and Palestine was but a fragment of her vast dominions, the future of earth was being moulded, not in the imperial city, but by a peasant of that insignificant province. In view of the historical antecedents, there is nothing wonderful in the man or the community that models its life after the Bible pattern, finding that the legislation is a model of wisdom and of beneficence. But our Lord did not say that he who did the will of God was to find out that the teaching was wise or good, but that he was to know that the teaching came from God. This discovery of the supernatural origin of the Word, this higher evidence of the authenticity of Scripture, is the wonderful thing in this statement of our Lord's. He does not teach that the mere performance of the things commanded will produce this result; but he does teach that if a man's heart be set on doing the will of God, this supranatural divine illumination comes. This divine illumination is the miracle of grace. It is a part, but not the whole, of the Christian consciousness. It has been much neglected by the individual Christian, and has been almost always practically ignored by the church; but it rises above faith. Faith gives us certainty where reason may fail us; but the Christian consciousness turns faith into sight. He does not believe that the Word is from God. He knows it.

By the genuineness and authenticity of the Scriptures must the Word stand or fall in the presence of that criticism which will not acknowledge the function of faith or of Christian consciousness. On such unbelievers we can still bring to bear the external and internal evidence in favor of inspiration. The external evidence can prove that almost all our New Testament was produced by the age to which it professes to belong; that for the most part it is the word of the living witness, and not the compilation of dim tradition. But external evidence by itself can never be proof positive of the divine origin of the Bible. The internal evidence will satisfy certain types of mind as a sufficient proof of the superhuman origin of the Bible; and the external and internal evidence combined will to many minds be a satisfactory proof of inspiration. But this mode of proof is confined to the scholarly few. Our Lord does not limit his promise to any select group. He does not say, if any man wills to do his will, and then pursues a certain course of study, but if any man wills. The offer of illumination is as wide as is the offer of salvation. Two perennial miracles live yet in the church of God. The assurance of salvation — of personal salvation — is the miracle of peace; and the certainty that God is speaking to us in his Book is the miracle of knowledge.

The keynote of the Reformation was faith. "The just shall live by faith." Faith *versus* works, and faith *versus* morality, was the great theme of the pulpits of Protestantism for a century after the Reformation. The legend of Rome was, "Do this and live;" the legend of Protestantism was, "Believe and live." It was natural and to be expected; but definite teaching concerning the knowledge of God, and what it is to know God, was conspicuously absent. The Confession of Faith, the Thirty-nine Articles, and the Catechism unite in having very little to say on this head. Knowledge was confused with and identified with faith. In the Shorter Catechism of the Westminster divines occurs the question, What is faith in Jesus Christ? It is a fundamental question, and the answer to it is as nearly perfect as we can imagine uninspired language to be: but alongside of it should have been such a question as, What is the knowledge of God? How many sermons in Protestant pulpits have been preached from Isa. viii. 2: "By his knowledge shall my righteous servant justify many." Jesus himself said that it was life eternal to know God. Christian consciousness has been obscured, because life-giving knowledge has been neglected or identified with faith, or treated as the synonym of information, and nothing more.

What is the province of Christian consciousness? It does not debate. It begins with "I know." Such questions as the mode of baptism and apostolic succession are in the field of ratiocination, not in the field of the Christian consciousness. Knowledge, and the processes of knowledge, in so far as the will and mind of God can be found in us, is the field given to us. God gives wisdom liberally, and does not scorn us for our need of it. This is not the talent which we must occupy, but it is the gift that occupies us. It is a constituent element of our Christian consciousness.

Christ is with his church always, to the end of the age, but only in so far as he is in the hearts of some or all of its members. Faith moves mountains, but Christian consciousness knows that this mountain is in God's way. Christian consciousness draws the people of God together in spite of the very definite reasons which they have for keeping apart from each other.

Man was made in the image of God. By his fall he lost communion with God, but he did not lose the likeness. It has not yet been demonstrated that any man is wholly devoid of the religious consciousness. This is at once a more scientific and a more satisfactory expression than the "light of nature." May not the salvation of the heathen be determined more by the God consciousness that is in him than by any reasoning that he has been able to do "from nature up to nature's God"? It is the religious consciousness, and not speculations concerning the attributes and the works of God, that must enable a man to escape judgment by judging himself. There are certain moral and ethical standards into which man has entered by the processes of reason; but there are moral and ethical dogmas which have come, as it were, out of a clear sky. Spontaneous generation in morals or ethics is as unthinkable as is spontaneous generation in matter; but the consideration of this topic, and its relation to consciousness, will come under the head of evolution in morals. It cannot be too deeply impressed upon our minds that there is no necessary conflict between the authority of Scripture and the religious consciousness. On the contrary, that German school to which reference has been already made, after drifting from the orthodox view of inspiration, has found the way back to reverence for the Word by their Christian consciousness. In one of the best of our religious weekly newspapers, which need not be named, an article appeared on the Christian consciousness, in which it was charged with being an excuse for heresy, and with being the ally of the higher criticism. Such an utter misapprehension of the nature and province of the Christian consciousness can scarcely be imagined. So far, it has counteracted the evil effects of what we may call heresy. The higher criticism is a detail of scholarship, and it has neither more nor less connection or affiliation with the Christian consciousness than any other department of scholarship has.

There is a trinity of illumination, — the light of revelation, the light of the religious consciousness, and the light of nature. God is the creator, the Holy Spirit the inspirer, and Christ in us the revealer. In the past the church has been undignified, timid, and apologetic when charged by her enemies with her changes of front on questions of ethics, of morals, and of interpretation. The right conception of the Christian consciousness should make the church glory in her changing, in her development, and in her elasticity. Those philosophers who are not inclined to introduce any theological or supranatural element into their conceptions of man's moral and ethical development have an ideal which they worship after a fashion. They maintain that the good deeds and the good thoughts of men have come from their aspirations after an ideal. We accept it all and go farther. Our ideal has become real to us in Christ. He is not only our hero and example and leader, but we have a consciousness of him. He is found in us, and we are found in him.

It is significant that, in the eighteenth century, when the pulpit contented itself with preaching moral essays, the majority of the philosophers of the same century were determined that theology should not have any place in their systems of moral philosophy. Locke, Shaftesbury, Hobbes, Hume, Bentham, and Kant are all at one in this respect; and it was almost the only point on which they were agreed. They had a very imperfect conception of religion, and for this the then current religious teaching was responsible. It was a cold, formal externalism. It had no inner life. There was no Christian consciousness. There was a God in heaven, whose business it was to deal out rewards and punishments in a fatherly or in a vindictive fashion, as the preacher happened to feel; but the yearning love of God for man and man's apprehension of God, were obscured. Hume's utilitarianism, or Bentham's greatest good of the greatest number, or Kant's imperative, was really a better scheme of the moral world than was the Dryasdust formalism of the church, in which there was no Christian consciousness, and very little of Christ as Jesus the Messiah.

CHAPTER II

THE DIGNITY OF MAN

The growth of the Christian consciousness was retarded from the fact that it placed dignity on man as the child of God. The Reformation theology had a tendency to an austerity which gave undue prominence to one side of the truth. That Adam fell from the estate wherein he was created by eating the forbidden fruit; that all mankind, descended from him by ordinary generation, sinned *in* him and fell with him in his first transgression; that the sinfulness of our estate consists in the guilt of Adam's first sin, in the want of original righteousness, in the corruption of our whole nature, together with all actual transgressions which proceed from it; that no mere man since the fall is able perfectly to keep the commandments of God, but doth daily break them in thought, word, and deed; that every sin deserves God's wrath and curse, both in this life and in that which is to come, — may all be doctrinally sound, and may be supported by proof texts; but it is a little depressing, and it gives humanity the gloomiest possible view of itself. Nor is the gloom dispelled by the unfolding of the plan of redemption; for, while our soul shrinks at the universal loss and ruin, we are told that God, " having out of his mere good pleasure, from all eternity, elected *some* to everlasting life, did enter into a covenant of grace to deliver them out of their estate of sin and misery, and to bring them into an estate of salvation by a redeemer." It is a depressing view of the truth, and it led to a conventional habit of self-depreciation that was not always sincere. The Penitential Psalm fits the case of the adulterer and murderer, and is an appropriate hymn for the condemned cell on the morning of an execution; but it may be used in a morbid fashion. It is true that in these days there is a tendency to the other extreme, and the " only believe," " trust him," " take him," of certain phases of revivalism, but not of all evangelists, ignore repentance unto life, and belittle restitution; but the older setting and statement of the truth belittled man. Granting that it is technically correct to say that all mankind by the fall lost communion with God, are under his wrath and curse, and so made liable to all the miseries of this life, to death itself, and to the pains of hell forever — it is, after all, only a half-truth. If man lost the Adamic communion, it was to find the Christ communion. If he is under God's wrath and curse, he is also under his love and mercy. If he is made liable to all the miseries of this life, he rejoices in hope. If he must encounter the pains of death, he also exultingly cries, "O death, where is thy sting?" If the pains of hell forever and forever lie before persistent choosing of evil rather than of good, he knows that full and free salvation is offered to him; and in his inmost soul he knows that the guilt of rejection must be his own guilt, and that no divine decree, no iron necessity in the nature of things, will prevent his attainment of everlasting felicity.

A departure from the right proportion and perspective of truth has all the evil consequences of error. Lecky, in his "History of European Morals," says, "But these exaggerations of human depravity, which have attained their extreme limits in some Protestant sects, do not appear in the church of the first three centuries. The sense of sin was not yet accompanied by a denial of the goodness that exists in man. Christianity was regarded rather as a redemption from error than from sin; and it is a significant fact that the epithet 'well deserving,' which the pagans usually put upon their tombs, was also the favorite inscription in the Christian catacombs. The Pelagian controversy, the teachings of St. Augustine, and the progress of asceticism, gradually introduced the doctrine of the utter depravity of man, which has proved in later times the fertile source of degrading superstition."

The Eighth Psalm is an exulting chant, and its theme is the excellence of God as manifested in the greatness of man. The central thought, so far as the greatness of man is concerned, is the fifth verse: "For thou hast made him a little lower than the angels, and hast crowned him with glory and honor." The false translation of our Authorized Version of this verse did injury to the truth, not only by its own error, but also by affecting our attitude to the New Testament doctrine of man. The Revised Version makes a very striking change:

"For thou hast made him but little lower than God." How comes so radical a change? The original word *Elohim* is the plural form of the word for God. The plural is by far the more common form of the word. It is the form used in the first chapter of Genesis, and in the Decalogue. It means god, gods, objects of worship. This psalm is the only case in which the word is translated *angels*. The translators were doubtless inclined to this rendering by doctrinal considerations. It was out of harmony with the prevailing thought of the age, and it was in sharp contrast to those Scriptures which enlarge on the distance between God and man. The Authorized Version is unfortunate in its rendering of this word, because the psalm sees the glory of man in his being the lord of creation; but angels are not associated with any dominion over this earth of ours. They are ministering, not ruling, spirits. Man, in his present earth life, may be lower than the angels who serve God, and who are sent forth on errands of "supernal grace;" but man's inferiority to angels is not taught in the Scriptures. In his ultimate destiny he will be greater, for he will be the judge of angels (1 Cor. vi. 3).

On the other hand, it is universally admitted that it is only in a limited sense that we can appropriate the being but little lower than God. This has been felt by the great majority of expositors. Hengstenberg says, "The *Elohim* expresses the abstract idea of Godhead." In Zech. xii. 8, *Elohim* may be regarded as identical with, or as parallel with, the "Angel of the Lord;" but many regard the words as distinct images of the glory that was to come to the house of David. The most difficult passage, so far as the use of the word *Elohim* is concerned, is 1 Sam. xxviii. 13: and in this case it is to be noted that the Revision changes "I saw gods," into "I saw a god." Calvin's comment is: "*Parum abesse eum jussisti a divino et coelesti statu*"—lacking but little of the divine and heavenly, or an almost super-earthly dignity. Hengstenberg's translation is: "Thou makest him to want little of a divine standing." Our Authorized Version is a literal translation of the Vulgate: "*Minuisti eum paulo minus ab angelis.*" This is the same as the Septuagint. The Septuagint and the Vulgate had a good deal of weight with King James's translators, for the very sufficient reason that they knew Latin and Greek much better than they knew Hebrew; but they knew Hebrew too well to account for this translation being other than deliberate choice on their part. Luther's Bible was before them. He translates, as our Revision does: "*Du wirst ihn lassen eine kleine Zeit von Gott verlassen sein.*"

The reference in this psalm is to certain special privileges bestowed on man; but a broad, general truth is also indicated, which may be thus stated. Man is made in the image of God. This image has been defaced or marred, not lost or blotted out. It can be restored. The dignity of man is in his past, a divine origin; in his present, divine possibilities; and in his future, a divine destiny. The Christian consciousness contemplates its greatness not in any vainglorious fashion, but in reverential mood. It does not ignore the revealed contrasted littleness of which it is always profoundly conscious. "Verily every man at his best estate is altogether vanity" (Ps. xxxix. 5). "Man being in honor abideth not: he is like the beasts that perish" (Ps. xlix. 12. 20). And yet there is a perfect man whom we should study, and an upright man whom we should imitate. To-day man is saying, "Let us eat and drink, for to-morrow we die;" but when the to-morrow comes, light perhaps has shined into the gross soul, and he cries that he cannot live by bread only: he hungers and thirsts for every word that proceeds out of the mouth of God. Poets and moralists like to dwell on these contradictions and opposites of human nature. One exclaims, "How poor a thing is man!" while another declares that "Man is a pendulum, 'twixt a smile and a tear." Pascal says that "Man is at once the glory and the scandal of the universe." Shakespeare had this Eighth Psalm in mind when he wrote, "What a piece of work is a man! How noble in reason, how infinite in faculties; in form and moving, how express and admirable; in action, how like an angel; in apprehension, how like a god." Godlike apprehension is Christian consciousness.

These extremes of vice and virtue, of benevolence and malevolence, are peculiar to man so far as we know the universe. Heaven is the home of holiness and of every conceivable moral and spiritual excellence. In view of the fall of the angels, we dare not affirm that sin is impossible to every one of the citizens of the kingdom; but we know that sin cannot enter into heaven, and it cannot stay there. We associate the condition of the lost with that hardened impiety and continuance in sin which we call permanence in evil. The lower animals have good or bad traits, dispositions, tempers, and habits; but we do not attach any moral merit or demerit to their actions.

Science searches in vain for the missing links which will prove the ascent of the physical man from the manlike ape or from any other of the mammalia. But even were such missing forms discovered, we must find many other links to account for his intellectual and spiritual development. Theistic evolution demands the existence of God, and his activity in his universe. But at this point all agreement ends. Charles Kingsley was wise as well as witty when he said that evolution exalted God. He did not make all things, but he made them make themselves. Some theists are contented to find God at the beginning. They reason that we might be able to find the missing links between man and the ape, and go back by visible steps until we came to the simplest forms of animal life, to find a trustworthy bridge between the animal and the vegetable kingdoms. When we come to the lowest forms of organic life, let us discover that spontaneous generation which science has looked for in vain. Let the inorganic earth be simplified, resolved into its elements, nay, let them disappear. In the infinite there float two atoms, call them microscopic atoms, molecules of matter, star-dust, or by any other name. Who made them? Whence came they? Who endowed them with the promise and potency of the all to come? Who ordained that in the infinite spaces these wandering parents of suns and systems should meet? Who presided at the wedlock that was pregnant with the all to come? God.

It is quite conceivable that the theist who accepts evolution of this kind and degree may stop short when he reaches the summit of physical life in man, and say, " Thus far and no farther." The intellectual, the moral, and the spiritual are not to be accounted for by evolution. The physical man began with a full equipment. moral and spiritual, for the battle of life; and his intellect, if without the gathered knowledge of experience, was a man's intellect and not a child's. But while it is quite conceivable that the more extreme theistic evolutionists may take this position, as a matter of fact they accept the doctrine of evolution in the region of the intellectual and moral. This they try to accomplish without irreverence and without irreligion. Professor Drummond's "Ascent of Man" is an outstanding example and illustration, but we do not assert that Professor Drummond is a theistic evolutionist of the extremest kind. In the other extreme of theism and evolution, we have those who willingly admit the principle of evolution in a general way; but they also believe that God is in his world, exercising creative energy when and where he wills. Some are not prepared to grant the possibility of the physical man being the product of evolution; and many deny the possibility of evolution accounting for the gift of speech, or for reason, conscience, and worship.

The history of the beginnings of civilization can never be written from a subjective standpoint; for races, like individuals, can neither remember nor chronicle their own infancy. The earth is dotted with the sad mementoes of vanished races. Civilizations that had attained a certain height have been blotted out by the savage. In Mexico and in Peru the higher disappeared before the lower. This is also true of Greece and Rome so far as culture is concerned; but the barbarians who overran Southern Europe were cleaner morally than were the sensualists of Rome. But not only does history tell us of races that have been overcome by the valor and virtue of an otherwise inferior or ruder race, we also see in our world of to-day, in the Indian population of the United States, in the natives of the South Sea Islands, Australia, and New Zealand, races disappearing before a civilization that has endeavored in a more or less blundering way to be just to them, and before a Christianity which has given men and money freely for their betterment. But the treatment of the inferior or savage races by the conquering and colonizing races has been neither wise nor just. We kill them before we give ourselves time to elevate them in the scale of civilization. Eighteen centuries ago our ancestors were naked or hide-clad savages, living in dugouts, or in huts of the rudest description. Their food was wild fruits, and animals caught in hunting, supplemented by the scantiest husbandry. Their religion was a bloody idolatry which demanded human sacrifices. They were as low as Hottentot or American Indian or South Sea Islander of to-day. It may be affirmed that at this point the comparison ends. These rude forefathers of ours on British moors, by Danish shores, and in deep German woods, had latent capabilities very much superior to those of the savage races of to-day. This is simple assertion, nothing more. It took from six to nine centuries to christianize these ancestors of ours. It took twelve centuries to produce Chaucer and Wycliffe. It took fifteen centuries to produce the Reformation, Shakespeare, and Bacon. It has taken nineteen centuries to produce us of to-day.

In the last hundred and fifty years we have done more in discovery and in invention, in physics and mechanics, than was accomplished in the preceding centuries of our era; but the Greeks were our equals from a purely intellectual standpoint, and the Christians of the first three centuries were our equals in excellence of morality. The divine day in which nations are born contains more than twenty-four hours. The Mongolian or the Negro race may represent the highest culture and the purest religion a thousand years hence; for who can prophesy what the result may be when these now barbarous races have had our centuries of training. It may also be true that special causes stereotype certain races, and launch others on a downward career so inevitable that no help from without can avert their ruin. In considering the development and decline of races, the "survival of the fittest" explains nothing. It is the mere antithesis to the death of the weakest. What we want to know is the philosophy of the causes that produce fitness and weakness. We are wise after the event. This *ex post facto* reasoning is interesting and instructive in its way. We have histories sacred and secular, so far as themes and modes of treatment are concerned, and histories of the church, and histories of civilization in abundance. It is easy to reason that the invention of the art of printing, the discovery of America, the decay of chivalry, the growing power of cities and trades' guilds as the natural foes of feudalism, the dispersion of Greek speech and Greek learning by the fall of Constantinople and other causes, had a cumulative force which had to result in the Reformation. And we talk about the times making the man, and the man making the times. God makes the man. He dowers him with the Christian consciousness, and the peasant priest, the miner's son, stands before kings. It is the unexpected that happens. Take the case of Italy. The States of the Church were badly governed. The rest of the country was in even a worse condition, with the exception of the northern kingdom. The country was cut up into petty principalities. There was no constitutional government. Misrule and grave oppression everywhere except in the north. The ignorance of the masses was unspeakable. Brigandage came to the gates of almost every city in Italy. The ancient spirit seemed dead. The land of Petrarch and Dante, not to mention the greater names of those who flourished when the Cæsars reigned in Rome, had now become a by-word among the nations. There was no reasoning or prophesying of that breath of life at the mysterious touch of which Cavour, Garibaldi, and Victor Immanuel came forth to build up the united Italy of to-day.

Take another example, nearer to English speakers in interest though more remote in time. In the middle of the eighteenth century a kind of moral and spiritual torpor prevailed in Britain and America. The Reformation was two hundred years old; and the visible outcome of it, with the exception of an illustrious history, was ecclesiasticism and infidelity. In England the lower orders of the clergy were too often recruited from men who were utterly incompetent from a moral or a literary standpoint. In its more desirable livings, the church was, to the privileged classes, just what the army and navy was. — a good place for younger sons. Fielding, Richardson, and Smollet supplied the literature of polite society. There was a little more outward decency than in the time of the shameless vice of the period of the Restoration of Charles II., but gambling was common among both sexes in the best houses of the land. Bull-baiting, dog-fighting, and pugilism without gloves, were popular amusements; and intemperance was common among all classes of the community. In Scotland the era of moderatism prevailed. The pulpit was lax. Drunkenness was perhaps more common than in England. Conversion was sneered at by the greater part of the clergy. The voices that came from the pulpits, where the heroes and martyrs of the Reformation had thundered, were but passionless definition of doctrine, elegant rhetoric of the cool and collected kind, and a Dryasdust morality.

In America the Puritan fervor of New England had to a great extent disappeared; and in its place had come an awkward aping of fashion, state, and ceremony, which sat clumsily on men who were born to faith, but who had lost sight of their birthright in aping an unattainable culture. In the South there existed all the religion and all the morality that were possible where domestic slavery prevails, where the mixed color tells the story of the white man's licentiousness, and of the colored woman's degradation. In the North they were freethinkers. In the South they were freelivers; and occasionally a member of the chivalry sold his colored daughter into harlotry, when he was hard up, and occasionally he lost his offspring at a gentlemanly game of cards. There were illustrious exceptions. There were many Lots in these eighteenth century Sodoms. There were pious clergymen, and there were holy families. Purity and piety had not fled the earth entirely, but evil was rampant. Almost simultaneously on both sides of the Atlantic, men who were born leaders arose to champion evangelical religion. Great revivals and the birth of modern missions, home and foreign, were the immediate results.

Into one soul is born the thought that organized missions to the heathen nations was the will of God and the duty of Christian churches, and many missions arise. Into another comes the blessed thought to send leaves from the Bible over the earth, like leaves from some tree of life, — the first Bible society is formed, and many follow in its train. What is the genesis of these movements, and of the men who led them, nay, who originated them. It is easy to be wise after the event, and to philosophize as to the likelihood or necessity of some such movement just at such a time. There is a striking passage in Sir William Dawson's last book, "The Meeting-place of Geology and History," which deserves to be quoted as the deliberate opinion of an eminent thinker, who has devoted himself during a long life to the study of geology, but who is one of the few scientists who are also scholarly, sympathetic, and competent archæologists and critics of the Bible. In chapter viii., the subject of which is "The Palanthropic Age in the Light of History," he, *inter alia*, demonstrates that the testimony of history and of geology is in favor of the arts of civilization originating with great inventors, that society has at times advanced by leaps and bounds, rather than by a slow uniformitarian process. We quote the closing sentence of his argument. "It is true that Genesis represents its early inventors as mere men, albeit 'sons of God,' while they often appear as gods or demi-gods in the early history of the heathen nations; but the fact remains, that then, as now, the rare appearance of God-given inventive genius is the sole cause of the greater advances in art and civilization. Spontaneous development may produce socialistic trades' unions or Chinese stagnation: but great gifts, whether of prophecy, of song, of scientific insight, or of inventive power, are the inspiration of the Almighty."

In the preceding chapter, inspiration has been defined as " the gift of infallibility in the proclamation of moral and religious truth." It is evident that Sir William Dawson uses the word in a wider sense than that of our definition. He is in accord with the conventional use of the word. In this more general and popular sense, Shakespeare, and the first man who made a fire, and the first man who represented a sound by a written character, were all inspired; but in the higher sense, we confine the term inspiration to those whose words or thoughts came to them by the special afflatus of the Spirit, so that they were infallible teachers. In the combination of inspiration and revelation the writers of the sacred Scriptures stand alone.

CHAPTER III

THE DESTINY OF MAN

The Christian consciousness knows. It has moral certainty and spiritual assurance; but it does not make any claim to infallibility, even in its own peculiar province. The Scriptures are infallible, but there are two serious discounts to their practical infallibility. The first is as to what measure of certainty we have that this reading is that which was penned by its inspired author. An unnecessary prominence has been given to this possibility of error creeping in through human fraud and carelessness in translation and in transcription, by the prominence given to the " original autographs " in a recent deliverance of the General Assembly of the Presbyterian Church North in the United States. The second discount to the practical infallibility of the Scriptures as the rule of life arises from that diversity of interpretation concerning dogma and morals to which we shall have occasion to refer in subsequent chapters. While theoretically an argument might be made for the infallibility of the Christian consciousness, the doctrine is of little or no practical utility. Nothing is gained by proving the possibility of that which never occurs. We assume the position that the Christian consciousness is not always and necessarily infallible. It is not inspiration in the closer definition of the word; but it is inspiration, or it may be, of the more general kind as seen in the use of the word by Sir William Dawson. It often possesses all the joy of illumination; but it is oftentimes far more than illumination. It is the witness of the Spirit with our spirits concerning truth. It is both the wisdom revealed to us and in us. It is the supreme test of spiritual truth. We make the expression "spiritually minded" do duty for many things to which the New Testament does not apply it. Very often Christian consciousness would be the better expression.

When Carlyle wrote, "Nobler in this world know I none than a peasant saint," it was not because there was any patent of nobility attached to a combination of poverty and saintliness. There would really be much more to wonder at, and to esteem as noble, in finding earnest piety combined with very great wealth, or with earthly positions of honor and of power. It could not be that the association of saintliness with husbandry conferred special honor. None knew better than Carlyle that the humble tillers of the soil of his native land were of the lineage of confessors, saints, and martyrs. With the keen insight of the seer, he saw in the peasant saint one whose mind was a tribunal to which grand moral issues came for judgment. The rustic could stand among princes, for he could speak the imperative yea and nay in life.

The Christian consciousness puts great honor upon man. Christian revelation and scientific evolution unite in declaring that the world was made for man, and that man is the flower of all the centuries, and the lord of this visible creation. The end is not yet. Evolution cannot say that the processes of nature have reached their goal, and that now, or ere long, development is to give place to permanence. Evolution of the scientific kind distinctly repudiates this most unscientific assumption. Nor can evolution consistently affirm that man returns to dust, once more takes his place among elemental matter, and begins once more the mighty circle of life. It is as unscientific to suppose that evolution is a circle, as to suppose that it has reached, or can reach, an ultimate and permanent form. The more thoughtful evolutionists are asking the question, What comes next in the destiny of man? He watches the progress from cosmic dust to life in its lowest forms, but with the origin of life unsolved. From primitive life to the higher mammals is a chain from which links are missing, — from the ape to man the greatest, most obvious missing link of all, and then upward from the lowest savage to the wisest and best men of to-day. And what shall come next? Surely honor is put upon man. Here or hereafter there must be something in store for him who is made a little lower than God.

Physical science and invention and discovery have faith in the future. They look back but a century, and the many uses of electricity and steam are unknown. Only a hundred years ago, and many of those things which have become the necessities of our civilization were unknown. It is almost a certainty that more will be accomplished in the twentieth century than has been achieved in the nineteenth, and a hundred years from now they may truly affirm that the twentieth century has accomplished more than the nineteenth accomplished.

Social science has also her forward look. She sees the time when human life will be sweetened and lengthened by a wise hygiene; when the earth will be able to support all her children in positive comfort; when labor and capital shall not conspire against each other; when there shall be no darkest England, or nihilist Russia, or anarchist America; when the submerged tenth shall have been elevated into social comfort and contentment; when the saloon and the gambling-house shall be matters of history; and, above all, when the vision of the Hebrew seer shall be fulfilled, and men shall learn the art of war no more. Religion has her forward look. By faith's clear vision she sees the day when all the earth shall have heard the proclamation of the gospel, and when no man shall have to say to his neighbor, "Know the Lord;" when men shall no longer exalt this sect or that denomination, but when schism shall be healed, and we shall all be one on earth.

But material, social, and religious progress does not answer the question, "What is the next step in the destiny of man?" Evil may be diminished, though we cannot tear sin up by the roots. Many moral improvements may come by the cultivation of ethics, and by the development of social science; but personal holiness may not grow in like proportion. Moral or spiritual growth is not necessarily aided by our achievements in physical science. A man who can cross the Atlantic in five days is not one whit more of a man, is not cleaner of soul or purer in life, is no truer to friend and lover, than he who had to battle with wind and wave for thirty days to reach his goal. Paul's sermon on Mars' Hill would not have been more sublime if he had travelled to Greece on a steam-yacht. The hand that bent the yew bow was just as steady, and the heart as brave, as are his who handles the modern rifle. The telephone is a triumph of civilization, but is a doubtful aid to morals. We can suppose our social burdens lightened by wise legislation, our churches rejoicing in visible union, and the gospel proclaimed in all lands; and yet open and secret sin may abound, even while the grossness of it and the volume of it may be diminished. In a century we may make notable progress, and yet the destiny of man is still unsolved. Immortality is the only solution of the problem of the present life. Morality demands a future in which the cultivation of virtue and the pursuit of knowledge, that have been cut off by death, may be resumed. Truth demands its vindication. Justice declares that every man should face his record. The everlasting right beholds the imperfect administration of justice this side of the grave, and says that there must be a future in which wrongs shall be made right. All these natural, reasonable, and moral desires are part of our Christian consciousness. Science and religion occupy common ground as to the destiny of man. Science beholds him standing erect, the apex of creation's pyramid, at once the product, and the heir and the king, of all the ages; and she says, "He is crowned with glory and honor." The Christian sees Him who is invisible, and says, "Thou hast crowned him with glory and honor." Agnosticism admits that there is as much to be said for theism as against it. Atheism in any form is a diminishing quantity. The number of those who admit the existence and personality of God, the First Cause, is steadily growing. To-day there are many scientific thinkers who are not avowedly Christian, but who are more theistic than agnostic. The divine Word says, " God made man ; " the materialist says, " Man made God." The Word says, " God is from everlasting to everlasting;" the materialist says, " Matter is from everlasting to everlasting."

The science of evolution is not materialism. Science is keen-eyed as far as her vision will carry. She sees the mighty chain of life. Highest of the highest, alone in the completeness of His glory, is the Almighty First Cause. There are ministering spirits round his throne; but of them we are told little, and conjecture ever flies with broken wing. Next is man, — a motley group. At one end we find Washington, Cromwell, Shakespeare, Augustine, Paul, John the Baptist, and Moses. With them class all lovers of God and of their fellow-men, — the virtuous poor and the unselfish rich. We descend through the ranks of greed and lust and shame, of sorrow and of sin, until we reach the lowest of the low in the disgusting and ingenious vice of some great city, or among those who dance in glee at the cannibal feast in darkest Africa.

But the Salvation Army goes down into the slum; and this almost bestial man is clothed and in his right mind, living cleanly, and learning to think cleanly. The missionary goes to the cannibal village: and ere long some of these cannibals are transformed, and they pray to the unseen Father, — they know God. They have Christian consciousness. Science looks upon the manlike ape next to man in nature's descending scale, and sees no soul, no speech, no conscience, and no shame. They will not eat their own kind; they are not cannibals. They will fight with each other, or with other animals; but there is no devilish ingenuity of cruelty, and no skill in torturing, to which western Christian civilization had resort, not so very long ago, and which flourishes in China to-day; but science sees divine possibilities in these men who to-day are in some respects worse than brutes, and her solemn verdict is, that man is nearer to God than he is to these apes. Nearly three thousand years ago, David the poet sang the greatness of the Creator manifested in the greatness of the creature, and said, "Thou hast made man a little lower than God." The dream and the hope of the best science of to-day sit at the feet of this sure word of revelation.

The destiny of man is a future of divine possibilities. In Eden the tempter came and said, "Ye shall be as God," as the Revised Version puts it; but the suggested act was immoral, and the result was fatal. It was the true goal by a wrong road. Sometimes the religious consciousness is very low. Man has no language of the spiritual life but a cry; but the cry has been for knowledge of God, for likeness to God. As religious culture advances, our watchword is not so much, "Heaven our home," as it is, "God our Father." The highest aspiration of the child of God is not to escape a condition of loss and suffering, or even to gain a condition of bliss and reward, but it is to become like God.

But who shall bridge the gulf between God and man, between humanity and divinity? Here is another missing link. Hitherto the science of evolution has searched, and searched in vain very often, for the missing links in the ascending series of creation. But there are three great missing links; and could these be found, every other gap is a question of detail, and might be left to time. The first missing link is that which is between the inorganic and the organic, between death and life. Spontaneous generation has not been proved. We must go back to the Word of life: "Let the waters bring forth;" "Let the earth bring forth." The second missing link is that which connects the animal life of the brute with the soul life of man. We search in vain until we fall back on the divine cosmogony, and learn that God breathed into his nostrils the breath of life, and man became a living soul. The third and last missing link is that which connects man with God. We cannot find it in physical development. Suppose that by purity of life and knowledge of hygiene, man were to get back to the length of days of the antediluvians. This is not becoming like Him with whom one day is as a thousand years, and a thousand years as one day. He cannot expect to find it by any growth in knowledge; for the pleasant pain of growing knowledge is, that each secret we wrest from nature reveals new regions of the unknown. The development of this missing link is spiritual. It has to do with likeness. Man who has borne the image of the earthly must take on the image of the heavenly. How is it to be accomplished? There are two factors to evolution or development of species. The first is the innate or inherent energy; and the second is the environment, which develops the stream of tendency, and provides for the survival of the fittest. Revelation fulfils the demands of science. It declares that man has this innate or inherent energy, for he was made in the image of God. The second demand is fulfilled by Christ, who is our environment. We can be found in him.

With the profoundest reverence it may be affirmed that at this end of the process there is not a missing link. It is found in Christ, who clasps humanity with one hand and divinity with the other. He took our humanity on him, that we might take his divinity on us. We are children and heirs with him. He is our elder Brother. God never gives empty titles. "Behold what manner of love the Father hath bestowed on us, that we should be called sons of God."

Science, if true to evolution and development, must point to a development of man beyond his present place and power.[1] As has been said,

[1] This view is not held by Mr. Huxley. In one of his more recent utterances, the Romanes lecture for 1893, he says: "The theory of evolution encourages no millennial anticipations. If, for millions of years, our globe has taken the upward road, yet some time the summit will be reached, and the downward route will be commenced. The most daring imagination will hardly venture upon the suggestion that the power and the intelligence of man can ever arrest the procession of the great year.

"It is true that science bears witness to the occurrence of cataclysms and catastrophes in the past; and the thing that has been may be again. It does not require the most daring imagination to picture the gradual or rapid approach of another glacial period, or of another period of extreme, more than tropical, heat. Even if bearable, they would alter the conditions of human life; and in that combat between the microcosm and the macrocosm, — that is, between the ethical and the cosmic force, — the cosmos would regain all the ground that has been lost." All this may be granted. It does not affect the destiny of man. Other races of men may have preceded the Adamic race, but we have no more moral relation to them than we have to the inhabitants of Venus. We have the Flood in the past, concerning which the eminent scientist, Sir William Dawson, finds geological testimony which corroborates the Biblical account, and the Nineveh tablet gives archæological indorsement. This catastrophe was a new departure for the human family. In 2 Peter iii. 5-13 we have an account of a cataclysm to come, and modern science admits that it is quite possible; and this also will end the earth life of man. We need a future for our evolution of man. Mr. Huxley's physical and intellectual progress meet the case only in part. Science gropes after immortality; revelation declares it. John Fiske, in his " Destiny of Man," says that " The doctrine of evolution does not allow us to take the atheistic view of the position of man." This essay and its sequel, " The Idea of God," by the same author, deserve far more attention than they have received. They state with scrupulous honesty the progress and the limitations of the scientific theist; and viewed from the standpoint of Christian belief they are among the most significant utterances of science in this generation.

Science declares that man at his best is nearer to the divine than to the brutal, and it also declares that at his worst he has the inherent power to rise to his best. Revelation declares that God has made him but little less than God, and has crowned him with glory and honor. Science demands efficient causes for phenomena. Revelation points to the original God image, and then to Him who was at once the Son of God and the Son of man.

view is in accord with the testimony of revelation to the past, and also to the future, of the earth.

The destiny of the brute is beyond and outside of any volition or plan on its part. Man's destiny, in a very important sense, is in his own hands. There is a royal road to his highest development. It is by Him who is the way.

Christianity asserts the dignity of man. It declares that a believer has been born again by an incorruptible seed, by a living and abiding ever-continuing word of God. He is in present possession of eternal life. Is not Christian consciousness natural and to be expected? Would it not be strange if this son and heir should be so estranged from his Father that there was no sympathetic knowledge between them? The unused power shrinks, shrivels, and weakens. This is true in the physical, the intellectual, and the spiritual. Is our Christian consciousness atrophied by disuse?

CHAPTER IV

THE EVOLUTION OF MORALS

THE consideration of the influence that the Christian consciousness has upon the development or evolution of morals, ethics, and doctrine, is to a certain extent influenced by the use which has already been made of it. As has been stated in the first chapter, Schleiermacher's position is, that religion consists properly in feeling. This is with him a fundamental principle. But those who reject the sensationalism of Schleiermacher will naturally be led to reject his assertion that we have an immediate consciousness of the divine, — a God consciousness. The attempt of the Ritchslian school to reconcile supranaturalism and rationalism is the chivalry of dogmatics when looked at from one point of view; but when the inspiration of Scripture is yielded as a lost cause, so far as its present lines of defence are concerned, only to be rescued by the Christian consciousness, orthodoxy naturally and properly takes alarm, and of course regards with suspicion the Christian consciousness which rescues the doctrine that ought not to have been abandoned.

In the *Andover Review* of October, 1884, there appeared a paper by Professor George Harris, entitled, "The Function of the Christian Consciousness." This article was a defence of, and a plea for, the so-called Andover theology, which for various reasons, into which it is not the province of the present work to go, was much more prominently before the public then than it is now. The points which Professor Harris makes and elaborates are: —

I. "The Christian consciousness gives certainty to the individual concerning the truth of Christianity."

II. "Another exercise of the function of the Christian consciousness is the progressive development of theology."

III. "The relation of Christian consciousness to the Bible."

It was natural, and to be expected, that in the then active stage of this particular phase of the controversy, criticism of this article was at once prompt and general. Dr. Francis Patton criticised it in the *Independent;* and it is scarcely necessary to add that it was keenly and trenchantly done. The Rev. Dr. Behrends, in the *Congregationalist*, also appeared as the champion of orthodoxy as opposed to the newer school at Andover. Their contention and their fear was that the supreme authority of the Scriptures was endangered by the functions ascribed to the Christian consciousness by Professor Harris. Nor were they without reason for their assertion, for the third division of the paper in question is lacking in precision of statement. The general impression which the reader who tries to follow the discussion with all possible judicial candor receives, is that Professor Harris used the "Christian consciousness" to support Andover theology, and that the critics who have been named, as well as others, were prejudiced against the doctrine of Christian consciousness because of the use to which it had been put. There is no need for alarm. The Christian consciousness of the individual is from God. The collective Christian consciousness of the church is from God. Our philosophy of consciousness is put in various forms by different schools. Christian consciousness will be the subject of debate as to mode of origin, essence, and functions, just as inspiration or conscience is: but the individual or the church that wills to do the will of God can never be led by the Christian consciousness into radical error of doctrine or of conduct.

What is our standard of Scripture interpretation? The Roman Catholic says, My standard is the church. I can rest in blessed satisfaction. The church tells me what to believe and what to do. The great councils have issued their decrees. Emergencies may arise, but the official head of the church is officially infallible. He thinks he has not much need for the Christian consciousness: but his child dies after a few struggling moments of life. In the hurry and excitement of the moment the sacrament of baptism has been neglected. This tiny morsel of mortality, this unbaptized babe, is to suffer eternal deprivation and disqualification because of this; and when he and the mother and the other more fortunate children are safely gathered on the other side, this frailest blossom of the parent tree is to be banished eternally. Christian consciousness rebels and doubts, and hopes against hope, and finally believes better than the church's creed. In these more enlightened times Roman Catholics have so many opportunities of taking knowledge of the Christlike lives of some of their Protestant friends, that the doctrine concerning the damnation of heretics has undergone a modifying process. The Christian consciousness demanded it.

Protestant denominations may be said to assert that their standard of Scripture interpretation is neither church nor creed nor teacher. Each and every one is to search the Scriptures. What do I think about Christ? The Scriptures testify of him. The duty which God requires of man is obedience to his revealed will; and the Word of God is the only rule to direct us. Theoretically this sounds beautiful, and savors of a large freedom; but the Protestant sometimes finds that his denomination is a close corporation. The Confessional symbols interpret the Scriptures, and the General Assembly or the Conference or the Association interprets the Confessional symbols; and these interpretations, which determine who are orthodox, who need discipline, and who deserve expulsion, are the voice of a majority, great or small, — a majority swayed by the heat of debate, the chronic rivalry of individuals and of parties, by the bitterness of political strife, or by the pecuniary interests involved, and often by the avowed determination to ignore the Christian consciousness as a dangerous and misleading factor. It is easy to reply to this, that it magnifies the admixture of error and human frailty which inheres in all man's work, but that these deliberations and decisions are reached by godly men, who believe in, and have prayed for, the Spirit's presence and power. Most gladly is all this conceded; but history is history, and the tyranny of overbearing majorities is only equalled by the divisive courses of stubborn minorities. In much of our ecclesiastical business and doctrinal controversy we almost expect to find men stubborn when they are in the right, and sublimely obstinate when they are in the wrong. It is no argument in favor of a condition of things to say that it has always been so; and to say that the thing that has always been is the will of God is a mixture of blasphemy and of fatalism. Surely there can

be a better way. The consideration of what
the Christian consciousness has accomplished
will give hope concerning the future. It is
desirable to enter upon this investigation with
the spirit of true philosophic inquiry. We
are not immediately concerned with the relation which the Christian consciousness bears
to this doctrine or to that. The outcome may
be for or against this creed or that denomination. It may help, or it may antagonize, the
new theology or the higher criticism, or it
may have no effect on either of those phases
of doctrine.

It is also desirable to bear in mind that
the common Christian consciousness is that consensus concerning doctrine, morals, or ethics
which is held by each and every Christian.
While this is the strict definition, we usually
call that the common Christian consciousness
which is the common or predominant thought
of the followers of Christ. It is self-evident,
that, while the consensus of a bare majority
or of a considerable minority may be regarded
as a form or phase of Christian consciousness,
we cannot regard it as being *the Christian consciousness* concerning the point in question.

The genuineness and authority of Christian consciousness cannot be settled by a majority vote.

It is desirable to consider the relation of the Christian consciousness to the evolution or development of morals and ethics, apart from its relation to the development or evolution of doctrine. What is meant by the expression? Is there such a law in nature as

THE EVOLUTION OF MORALS?

Evolution accounts for the growth of the intellectual and moral as well as for the physical man. Herbert Spencer, in his illustrations of universal progress, says, "Little as from present appearance we should suppose it, we shall yet find that at first the control of religion, the control of laws, and the control of manners, were all one control. However incredible it may now seem, we believe it to be demonstrable that the rules of etiquette, the provisions of the statute book, and the commands of the Decalogue, have grown from the same root." Now, the very doctrine which Mr. Spencer introduces with the unavoidable conscious self-importance of even a modest discoverer, and tells us how incredible it may seem, is exactly the belief of many earnest Christians. Manners, law, and morals have grown from the same root, have been bruised by rough handling, their kinship is becoming more and more apparent. In well-ordered Christian families, "law, religion, and morals" do spring from the same root. In this lies our hope that the state and the world will yet more and more resemble a holy family. Mr. Spencer evidently takes no small amount of satisfaction in discovering three fruits from one root. We, too, are satisfied, but not quite so much amazed as he is, for the Tree of Life has twelve manner of fruits. In sympathy with the position of Herbert Spencer, George Henry Lewes, in his "Problems in Life and Mind," says, "The great desire at this age is for a doctrine which may serve to condense our knowledge, guide our researches, and shape our lives, so that conduct may be the result of belief." Mr. Lewes saw no hope of getting such a doctrine from revealed religion. His hope was in a "religion founded on science." The Christian philosopher maintains that the Scriptures unfold such a doctrine; and Christian philosophy goes deeper than this distinguished doubter's, for it declares that love keeps the commandments, and he that wills to do His will knows the supranatural excellence of the doctrine.

The history of civilization and the history of morals form one great theme. Guizot, Buckle, and Lecky have the same story to tell, however different their motives and their manner of telling may be. It is, of course, with the development of morals in the Christian era that we are concerned. We have not to establish or prove the fact of this development. It is universally granted. In civil and religious liberty, in the amelioration of the penal code, in our thoughts regarding, and our treatment of, such questions as witchcraft, slavery, foreign missions, and temperance, we recognize the fact that great changes have occurred, and that great advances have been made. It is not so long ago that the slave-ship was carrying on a legitimate business, and that slavery was a most Christian institution. The clergymen of a hundred years ago had not begun to doubt the propriety of the habitual use of intoxicating liquors. We see more clearly than they did, and we wonder at the witch-burning, and the reckless, if legal, killing of men for so many crimes. We are able to look forward to the time when we shall have overcome many of the evils, and shall have got rid of many of the burdens, of our present social system. While the fact of development in morals is granted, the greatest diversity exists as to the cause or causes of man's progress. Long before there was any evolution theory with regard to physical life, evolution theories in morals were not only promulgated, but were also received with little question. Not until these theories were pushed to their legitimate conclusions was the alarm taken. The vague term EXPERIENCE was credited with all theoretical and practical progress in ethics. Scholars got into the habit of speaking of the inductive method as being the true and only cause of all progress in moral as well as in physical science. Many scientists scouted the bare idea of a superintending, adjusting, or interfering Providence finding anything to do in the physical universe of to-day; and, by an easy transition, they also refused to believe in a divine moral government and governor. But the moving of God out of his universe, either by denying his existence, or by removing him to the infinite height and solitude of the Great First Cause, that did not in any way shape or interfere with the destiny of man, did not solve the difficulty. What is the philosophy of, the key to, the satisfactory explanation of that human progress which we commonly term the process of civilization or development in morals?

Utilitarianism was credited with much developing power. We are told in the Bible that on a certain occasion when good men were assembled, Satan appeared also,[1] as indeed he usually does. He was confronted with the problem of accounting for virtue and for moral and spiritual excellence; and his reply was, "Doth Job fear God for naught?" He is the first and greatest of the utilitarians; and to-day we have the sneer about "worldliness and other-worldliness." The world did not require to wait for some revealed word of reply to this ingenious theory that virtue was begotten of selfishness, and that morality was a kind of insurance against wrath to come, whether in

[1] Job i. 6.

this or in some future state of existence. In his " Republic " occurs Plato's well-known criticism of Homer; and one fault which the great philosopher finds with the grand poet is that he recommends justice by the inducement of temporal rewards, and thus turns morality into prudence. In passing, let it be said that it was a delicately adjusted religious consciousness which scorned the idea of morality having no higher inspiration than prudence. He could discern with clearness many of what Sir James Mackintosh, in his " Progress of Ethical Philosophy," calls the "august and sacred landmarks that stand conspicuous along the frontier between right and wrong." Mr. Lecky affirms that utilitarianism leads to conclusions utterly and outrageously repugnant to the moral feelings. Here he stands with Plato against the arch enemy; but when he claims that general moral principles are revealed by intuition, are progressive, and that theological influences retard philosophical truth, we are not so sure as to what side he is on. Buckle's tests of growing civilization are the absence of persecution for religious opinion, and not going to war; but we naturally ask whether these so-called tests are the causes or effects of civilization, or are they not more properly to be regarded as parts of civilization or of morality? Buckle gives supremacy to the intellect, but Comte to the heart. There is much that is attractive in the religion of humanity which we can learn from, without worshipping humanity.

The "struggle for existence" is not as new a thought in social as it is in physical science. Hesiod said that society was constructed on a basis of competition; that a principle of strife which makes potter foe to potter, produces all honorable enterprise. Physical progress is secured by the destruction of unsuitable forms, their weeding out, and by the cultivation of the successful; that is, by the survival of the fittest. Nature wants nothing but a fair field and free play for the strongest. Trade is competition, a struggle for existence. The survival of the sharpest is not always the survival of the fittest, from the moral, or even from the ethical, standpoint. Moral evolution demands a fair field and fair play for the weakest. It does not break the bruised reed. The Christian sociology of to-day, as a philosophy, is empiric simply because ethical science is so vague; but in many of the practical outcomes of it, such as the institutional church, college residences among the lowly, and the rescue work of the Salvation Army, it is saved from all nomenclature by being the imitation of Christ, who from the standpoint of even those who deny his divinity, was the greatest, most radical, and most far-reaching reformer that has ever appeared on earth.

F. D. Maurice's "Social Morality" created a good deal of interest when the lectures were delivered and afterwards published. It has historical insight and elevated moral sentiment, and a generous enthusiasm for virtue; but the questions at issue now were not on the field of discussion when he wrote. He cannot escape the environment of Oxford and of the State Church. He goes out of his way to make a plea for aristocracy and for a hereditary legislature. He sees advantage in the inheritance of patrician and plebeian, and with proud humility writes himself a plebeian. Of course not a few of his audience were self-complacent juvenile patricians. We are not so much concerned about whether the individual or the family constitutes the unit of social life, as to how social life is to be developed in the unit and in the family. Hume remarks that "the principles upon which men reason in morals are always the same, though the conclusions which they draw are often very different." This was true in Hume's time; it is not the case now.

The systems of moral philosophy had to account for the developments of virtue and of vice, but it was largely done as an abstract science. The metaphysicians and the moralists dissected the mind as anatomists dissected the body. They had their vivisection too, but it consisted chiefly in the relish with which rival schools cut each other up. The political economists imparted a human interest to moral philosophy which it did not before possess. Biology opened a new and very productive field in the study of man, morally and intellectually as well as physically. The comparatively new science of sociology was a study of moral and physical conditions, and it was also an active effort to remedy and to help. The philosopher in his study can tell us a great deal about the moral nature of man; but the study of the living organism Society by the man who works in college settlement, or in people's palace, or in some Salvation Army rescue work, gives opportunities of studying problems in life and mind and morals in concrete fashion. Those men who are combining culture with practical study of social conditions, and with practical efforts to help and to elevate, know that their work is of unusual significance in these days of communism, socialism, unrest, and discontent. Bellamy and his followers and imitators dream of a social future. Novelists weave their plots round the ways and means adapted to take some moral, intellectual, and social sunshine into darkest England. Slumming becomes a virtuous rage. Altruria becomes a country; and altruism, instead of being almost a philosophical term, becomes almost a household word. The active help was not the only manner in which the quickened social sympathy manifested itself. In the past, when a strike took place the general public looked on and grumbled when their own comfort was interfered with; but the general feeling was expressed by the words, "Let them fight it out." When the discontent became riotous, rebellious, and revolutionary, the policy was to give the dog a bone if you were not able to knock him on the head. Now all is being changed. Courts of arbitration are being discussed. Trades unions and organized labor generally are treated with respect. When a strike takes place, the right and the wrong of it are vigorously discussed. Eminent clergymen win the applause of all when they are the successful peacemakers. As is usually the case when money has to be raised and service rendered, much of the work, almost all of it, in fact, which looked to the better understanding of the miserable, and to their betterment in a permanent fashion, was done by the churches or by professedly Christian people. The evolution of ethics and morals had been expounded by non-Christian evolutionists. Materialist, positivist, agnostic, and humanitarian had all had their say; but the actual was, meanwhile, being done, not by the followers of these various schools, but by Christians, by the churches, by ladies living among the lowly, by scholarly young men from universities and theological seminaries, and by the soldiers, male and female, of the Salvation Army. It was high time that the evolution of morals should be treated from the point of view which religion supplies. Benjamin Kidd's able work on "Social Evolution" has attracted much attention. It has the merit of being so clear in its reasoning, and so lucid in its language, that it has already secured a wider audience than, as a rule, has been won by works of its class. It has been keenly criticised; but hitherto its principal positions have not been successfully assailed. He maintains that our civilization is founded upon an ultra-rational system of ethics. He bears repeated testimony to this immense fund of altruistic feeling. But, though he does not say it in so many words, the ultra-rational that makes for righteousness manifested by self-surrender must be inspired. The writer is in hearty sympathy and cordial agreement with almost all Mr. Kidd's argument: for his book has the merit of being an unbroken and well-sustained argument. That which it is the aim of this book to prove to be the law of the evolution in morals in relation to the Christian consciousness is not inconsistent with his theory of social evolution.

It is interesting that Professor Drummond's "Ascent of Man" should be almost contemporary with Mr. Kidd's "Social Evolution." This work has been severely criticised by the scientists, who are not satisfied with its Christian spirit; and it has been even more severely handled by Christian critics, because of alleged shortcomings. But meanwhile it has the winning manner of putting things which has made Professor Drummond so popular, and good people who read it are not hurt by it. His scheme of the development of morals appears at first sight antagonistic to Mr. Kidd's; but they are not really so very much opposed. The author of "Social Evolution" is not so much concerned about the genesis of the moral idea, as with the fact that religion has moral sanctions to spare, and that she does leaven society with these ultra-rational moral sanctions. Religion can give only that which is in the hearts of its votaries; not in the heart of each one, or in the hearts of all, but the predominant thought and feeling. His altruistic fund can never rise above the level of the Christian consciousness; or, since he avoids the term Christian, let us put it that his altruism, his ultra-rationalism of morality, is the manifestation of the religious consciousness. It may at first sight seem a contradiction; but perhaps the best way of indicating the relation of these famous books to each other is to note that there is some reason for Professor Drummond taking exception to some of Mr. Kidd's views, but there is no reason for which Mr. Kidd should oppose Professor Drummond's book in the interest of his own "Social Evolution."

CHAPTER V

THE CHRISTIAN CONSCIOUSNESS AND SLAVERY

The study of the evolution of morals is facilitated by taking some particular instance and example. We take human slavery because it has been universal, and, so far as civilization is concerned, it has passed into history. It is now a problem in ethics and in morals. In the earliest civilization, there were slaves of every kind. Sometimes the slavery was that of subject peoples engaged on great public works, or that of races laboring under the burden of a tribute of such exorbitant extent that they were slaves indeed to their conquerors; or it was domestic servitude. The slaves of the ancient world were not confined to that one race so much identified with slavery in modern times, but were captives taken in battle, purchased slaves, and the children of slaves, who inherited the bondage of their parents. When the condition of the slave was favorable, or even happy, it was because his owner was kind or indifferent, and not because he was protected by humane legislation. In the dawn of history the laws were made for freemen, and the servile class were wholly at the mercy of irresponsible owners. When laws began to be made, with regard to slaves, they indicate the unspeakable cruelty which preceded them. It was enacted that it would be wrong for a master to put his slave to death without securing legal permission, but that if he happened to kill a slave when chastising him, he was to be held innocent. When a slave became sick, and in order not to be put to the trouble of caring for him, he publicly abandoned him, and the slave recovered, the master could not claim him again. These laws show how miserable the condition of the slave was. Christianity did not do much to improve the condition of the slave, and the little that was done was accomplished very slowly. The serfdom of Europe was a modified form of bondage, and in the feudal system the mass of their retainers were the practical slaves of the barons. Liberty came slowly, not so much from servile insurrection, as from the growth of cities and the freemen sheltered by their walls, and from the power that the yeomen learned that they possessed when princes fought, or barons were arrayed against the king, and the king against his barons.

When slavery came to an end in Europe, it was from natural causes. Neither church nor state had any convictions on the question. No moral issue was raised; and almost immediately the pious and the thrifty, as well as the adventurer and the vagabond, became interested in the slave-trade to the colonies beyond the seas. Nor were negroes from Africa the only victims. In November, 1648, a contemporary authority tells this story: "The two charitable merchants that have bought four hundred Christians to send beyond the sea for slaves, were brought before the House of Lords, to show by what authority they were to transport them, who, upon examination, produced an order of the House of Commons, and being demanded what qualities they were of, they answered that they were all common soldiers and Scots, not one Englishman among them; then says one, it will be enough: they are as much slaves as ever they can be. But what! Have they sold none away but Scots? How many hundred poor apprentices of London have they sold perpetual slaves to the Turks, or sent to plantations where they shall not be half so well used as are here our horses and oxen!" There is a vein of sarcasm in this contemporary account of the doings of this famous Parliament. It goes on to tell that these white slaves being only Scots, and the Lords, not knowing but that the Commons would sell them next, leave was granted. Just before attending to the speculation of these enterprising merchants, the Commons sent a message to the Lords, desiring their concurrence in sending the Catechism of the Westminster Assembly to the king at Carisbrooke Castle.

This was the Parliament which defeated the king, who in a few months was to be executed. It was altogether in control of Puritans, Independents, and Presbyterians. Need we be surprised at the readiness with which the American colonists in New England and in Virginia accepted slavery as a part of their social system? This Parliament, containing many men of eminent piety, and composed almost wholly of those who had ventured their lives in this successful struggle for civil liberty and for religious freedom, is not troubled at all about the abstract morality of slavery; but it was scarcely fair to sell London apprentices into slavery, because these apprentices were their own kith and kin. As for those common soldiers and Scots. who had been fighting on the wrong side, that was another question.

John Bacon of Barnstable, Mass., died in 1731, leaving a "negro wench," Dinah, as a chattel to be disposed of by will; and this will was to the effect that Dinah should be sold, and the proceeds of the sale were to be devoted to the purchase of Bibles. This in New England! And in old England good men gave God thanks for the successful ventures of their slave-ships on the African coasts. We smile at these incidents, and marvel at the moral obtuseness which they indicate; but not so great a blot is this on the eighteenth century as is the taxation of harlots and of sellers of strong drink in the nineteenth century. A late senator from Illinois introduced a bill to legalize the education of children by the profits of the liquor traffic. Moses was not a slave, but he was of a nation of slaves, whose freedom he secured; and we do not know that he had any theoretic objections to slavery as a system, and yet his statutes decree that the price of a dog or the wages of sin were not to go into the Lord's treasury. His aesthetics are as remarkable as are his ethics.

There was a time when slavery was considered right by the Christian churches, and by Christians as individuals. We can imagine that the degradation of use and wont made the slaves themselves acquiesce in the state of things. Even on moral grounds the man who is a slave cannot bemoan the radical injustice of his lot, so long as he, without scruple, would enslave the enslaver if he had the upper hand. Every student of history and of the Bible knows that there was a time when, humanly speaking, slavery in and of itself was not opposed to human or even to divine legislation. Just as certainly as there was a time when every body thought that SLAVERY WAS RIGHT, just as certainly there came a supreme moment when there came to some soul the truth that SLAVERY WAS WRONG. And of course the thing that is morally wrong cannot prove a permanent advantage to the state, to society, or to the individual. Now, the question is, How came this new thought into the world? What is the genesis of it? It may be, and it is frequently replied, "This is the result of evolution in morals. It comes from observation and experience." Mr. Kidd tells us that the altruism with which society was equipped by. religion, the ultra-rational morality, was the axe that was laid at the root of the tree of slavery. Professor Drummond exalts the evolution of love, and self-sacrifice for love's sake, and this provided the altruistic feeling before which slavery was doomed.

It may be granted that the development or evolution theories of these two eminent thinkers, as well as the theories that have been advanced by Huxley, Spencer, and others, account satisfactorily for the gradual amelioration of the condition of the slave; but they do not account for the reversal of the world's thought. To own a slave is right; to own a slave is wrong. This is a new thing in morals. Spontaneous generation in morals is just as unthinkable as is spontaneous generation in matter. It has been the custom, both in and out of the pulpit, to compare the advances in morals with those discoveries and inventions which are producing such constant change upon the life of man. The changes in the outward life are not without their reflex action upon the inner life. There is a superficial reasonableness in such comparisons. The discovery is the finding of the treasure which has been lying in the lap of nature, waiting the appropriating hand of man; and the invention is the combination and adjustment of existing principles or laws to produce a new result. We may call the new thing in morals a discovery, and declare that it has always been lying in the nature of things, and in the revealed Word, waiting for the eyes that were yet to see it; or we may call it an invention, and affirm that it is in harmony with that law from Heaven for life on earth, to which as to a divine measure we bring it. There is, however, an essential difference. It is one thing to discover or to invent in the physical, to detect the law, or to combine the laws to produce a new result, and quite another thing to discover or to invent, if such terms are admissible, the truth which is a direct and emphatic reversal of the truth which has been accepted in all time as in harmony with morality as a science. And this holds true whether or not our system of morality acknowledges the Word of God as its ultimate standard.

We do not know who was the first to utter this new truth. We do not know that he was in a position to reason from observation and experience. It may be maintained that abstract reasoning on theoretic justice, excited by the recital of experience on the part of others, or by witnessing the evils of slavery, might be the producing cause. Is it not nevertheless true that the Christian consciousness, the divinity in the man, is the womb, the theatre of the gestation time of this new birth of truth? Like the Christ of extraordinary parentage, both human and divine, it is a fountain-head of good. This new thing in morals is not wholly made of things that do appear.

Who was the father of this truth?[1] Who can tell? It may be asked why those whose names and memories are forgotten should be chosen as the authors of great truths? We do not know. We have not yet mastered the prin-

---

[1] It may be claimed that moral births are the begotten of the times, and not of the individual. This is really no objection. In the moral universe there must always be "A fulness of time." The Christ has a forerunner, and disciples who accompany and follow him. That a new truth in morals should be revealed simultaneously in widely separated localities does not disprove its revelation, but a case of simultaneous revelation has not yet been proved."

ciples of divine selection and election. We do not know for what reason Mary was chosen as the mother of our Lord. We do not know what was the nature or measure of the fitness that Christ saw in each of the Twelve. Before Wilberforce, Clarkson, and Garrison, are Anthony Benezet, William Dellwyn, and Granville Sharp. Before them are more obscure names.

Samuel Sewall seems to have been the first in America to denounce slavery and the laws against witchcraft. He was born in England, 1652, and died in New England, 1730. In 1692 he gave his official sanction to the punishment of witchcraft; but five years afterwards he acknowledged his error. In 1700 he published a pamphlet. "The Selling of Joseph," in which he says that there could be "no progress in gospelling" until slavery was abolished. There are two points deserving attention in this case. The bondage of penal servitude made slaves of white men in the colonies at this time, and their servitude excited a consideration and compassion which would not be as readily given to an alien race like the negro. We can easily imagine that had the mixture of races been impossible on this continent, the slavery of the black race might have continued for a longer time before its final overthrow. The English people of 1648 had much more tender regard for London apprentices than they had for common soldiers and Scots. When quadroons and octoroons, and even those in whom the African taint was even still more attenuated, had to follow the mother's fate, the moral offence became more rank. It "smelled to heaven."

It is also of special significance to note that Samuel Sewall was just the man in whom we would expect a development of the Christian consciousness. Scholarly, refined, and pious, he used his great wealth in the doing of good. He fell into the prevalent error regarding the legal punishment of witchcraft; but when light came to him he publicly confessed his error. It will be admitted by all, that we have in him a man who willed to do the will of God. Why should not he be the man chosen to know the teaching on this matter? To be sure, he was only a voice crying in the wilderness, but the voice was the result of a divine persuasion and conviction. From 1700 to the day when Lincoln issued his famous proclamation of independence and freedom for the slave, was a long time. Nay, it was a long time from 1700 to 1792, when the first legal action in the direction of manumission was attempted in the country that was the first to free its slaves; but there was an unbroken chain of causation, although we may not be able to trace its sequence link after link.

Who were the predecessors of Samuel Sewall in holding this opinion that slavery was wrong, even though they were not moved to proclaim it to all the world? or into how many hearts did questions and doubts come as to the abstract right and wrong of it? Who can tell? We must beware of the easy and unphilosophical talk about the thing that is right in one age being wrong in another. Slavery was just as much a wrong in Abraham's time as was polygamy; but Abraham was not morally guilty, although he was a slaveholder and a polygamist. The existence of wrong is one thing, and the innocence of ignorant wrong-doing is quite another thing. We can trace the stream far back, but its living source we cannot find. Aristotle affirmed that slavery was part of the law of nature, but he admitted that some of his contemporaries denied this. But their denying that it was part of the law of nature does not prove that they regarded slavery as being immoral.[1]

It was not until 1792 that a bill was introduced into the British House of Commons, which had for its aim the gradual extinction of slavery; and forty-two years elapsed before its final extinction in Great Britain. In 1794 the French Convention decreed that all slaves in French territory should be free; and fifty-four years afterwards slavery was finally abolished in the dominions of France. Slavery was not entirely abolished in the Dutch colonies until 1863. The United States has a unique place with regard to slavery, which is worthy of special attention in the study of moral science, and also in the relation of the church to moral problems. When the agitation against this evil was active in England and in France, the sentiment against it in the United States was strong and full of hope. Washington declared that there was not a man living who wished more sincerely than he did to see a plan adopted for abolishing slavery, and he showed his sincerity to the end by leaving the great body of his

[1] See note on page 90.

slaves free. Jefferson was a slaveholder, and as early as 1774 he said, "The abolition of domestic slavery is the greatest object of desire in these colonies." It was he who proposed a constitution for Virginia, in terms of which all born after the year 1800 were to be free. Monroe's testimony was that slavery had "proved prejudicial to all the States in which it existed." Patrick Henry thus puts himself on record : " It would rejoice my soul that every one of these, my fellow-beings, was emancipated. . . . We detest slavery ; we feel its fatal effect; we deplore it with all the earnestness of humanity." These are not the sentiments of Northern men, but of Southern men ; and need it be added, that these opinions of their greatest men were echoed and indorsed by many of lesser name than they. After listening to these voices, would not any student of history have been justified in coming to the conclusion that slavery in the great Republic was doomed. Slavery was an evil inheritance from colonial times. The Declaration of Independence opened with a ringing sentiment as to the freedom and equality of men, and the possession by all of inalienable rights and privileges.

It was now a question of ways and means; but the doing away of slavery was a foregone conclusion. Years of marvellous prosperity followed. The young Republic became the great Republic; but slavery remained, and the number of the servile population increased rapidly. The immorality associated with domestic servitude was inevitable; and as the child followed the class, or rather remained in the class, of the mother, the strange spectacle was witnessed of men and women who were three-fourths, seven-eighths, and even fifteen-sixteenths, white blood, being bought and sold as merchandise.

More than half a century of religious activity followed along with this strange condition of affairs, and we had religious denominations that gloried in their orthodoxy and in their conservatism, and a society that was sensitive and punctilious on the score of personal honor. Washington, Monroe, Jefferson, and Henry were honored names, and the mention of them excited hearty enthusiasm in any public assemblage; but their feelings and utterances about slavery were ignored and forgotten. As might be expected, there was a change of front in the Southern estimate of slavery. A distinguished

Southern preacher, who wielded more influence in the South than any other man in his profession, preached a sermon at the end of the year 1860, in which he urged the maintenance of slavery for the following reasons: —

(1) As a duty to themselves, because their material interests were bound up in it.

(2) As a duty to their slaves, because the negro was a helpless being, requiring white protection and control.

(3) As a duty to the world which depended so much on Southern cotton.

(4) As a duty to God, who had appointed slavery, and whose honor was impeached, and whose cause on earth was imperilled, by the atheistic spirit of abolitionism. He said, " With this institution assigned to our keeping, what reply should we make to those who say that its days are numbered? We ought at once to lift ourselves intelligently to the highest moral ground, and proclaim to all the world that we hold this trust from God, to preserve it, and to transmit it to posterity, with the unchallenged right to go and root itself wherever Providence and nature shall carry it." In 1864, the " Narrative of the State of Religion," which it is

the custom to give before the General Assemblies of the Presbyterian Church, was given to the church in the South, and contained the following passage: "The long continued agitation of our adversaries has wrought within us a deeper conviction of the divine appointment of domestic servitude. . . . We hesitate not to affirm that it is the peculiar mission of the Southern Church to conserve the institution of slavery, and to make it a blessing both to master and slave." We have no right to question the personal honesty of these gentlemen, or the sincerity of their personal convictions. At the same time it is quite conceivable that the rancor of sectional strife and political feud fed the fire of their convictions.

The political economist has an argument of quite a different nature. He has figures to give us and stubborn facts. Eli Whitney invented the cotton-gin in 1793. His invention, supplemented by the inventions of Watt, Hargreaves, and Arkwright, converted slave-holding from a financially doubtful into a paying business. Slaves doubled in price. The cotton product of 1793 was ten thousand bales. In 1830 it was a million bales. The scoffer says that it very soon became apparent that slavery was a divine institution. While this was the state of affairs in the South, the more violent abolitionists were taking the church to task in the North. Some of them left the church because they could not find that Jesus or the Old or New Testament distinctly forbade slavery. Others left because the churches would not openly espouse their cause, and many of the wealthy conservative people threatened to leave if the church got mixed up in what they claimed to be a political discussion and question.

In a subsequent chapter the relation of the church to evolution in morals will be treated. It is not necessary to say whether the North or the South was right. Nor do we need to-day to go into the merits of the much-debated question, as to whether or not the Bible was in favor of slavery. To the oft repeated and ingeniously put arguments of Southern divines, the North had its reply; and a passage from Munger's "Freedom of Faith" may be given, which, while it appeared long after slavery became a dead issue, expresses in felicitous language the spirit of the rejoinder of Northern Christians to their brethren of the South:

"Humanly speaking, slavery could not be kept out of the Hebrew commonwealth; it was too early in the history of the world; but it was hedged about by strenuous laws, all merciful in their character, and of such a nature in their operation that slave-holding became unprofitable, and the system died out. Moses was wiser than this nineteenth century of ours. He sapped the life-blood of the institution by wise statesmanship; we drowned it in a sea of blood and fire, — blood from a million hearts, fire that touched the hearts of forty millions." All this is true, and well and eloquently said; but then it is quite venturesome to make comparisons between Moses and the nineteenth century. Moses had not to meet the case of Eli Whitney and his cotton-gin.

It is humiliating and suggestive that the line of cleavage on this question of slavery ran through all branches of the church, North and South. As an argument based on the letter of Scripture, and even on the spirit of it, or upon all the spirit of it that could be reached by argument, the position of the South was the stronger; and yet they failed, not only by fortune of war, but by the verdict of humanity.

The Christian consciousness was against slavery. There was no appeal from its final verdict. The thought born in some unknown soul, *To own a slave is wrong*, was a living thing. The Christian consciousness of that unknown founder and father of abolition grew until nation after nation broke the shackles from men's limbs. Those who would not bow to the Christian consciousness were ground in the mills of God.

"The blood-bought gold fell from the Spaniard's fainting
    hold,
And the Frenchman sunk to his Haytien grave,
Beneath the shout of the conquering slave."

Dr. Munger's eloquent words which have been quoted tell the experience of the United States in the mills of God. The British Empire was the first, and in some respects the greatest, sinner of all in the matter of slavery; but its repentance was manifested, not only by voluntarily freeing the slaves, but also by taxing itself so that the loss might not fall altogether upon the slave-owners, and also by her vigilance in suppressing the slave-trade in Africa and upon the high seas. But it was easier for Britain to be virtuous than it was for the

Southern States. The West India planters were but an insignificant portion of the Empire, and the British were cotton manufacturers while the Americans were cotton growers.

CHAPTER VI

THE CHRISTIAN CONSCIOUSNESS AS RELATED TO INTEMPERANCE, THE OPIUM TRADE AND GAMBLING

WHILE slavery affords an opportunity of studying the Christian consciousness as related to the evolution of morals as a reform that has been already, if but recently, accomplished, we have, in the use of intoxicating liquors as a beverage, an example of a new thing in morals which is yet subject to discussion. Presumably there never was a time when drunkenness was not considered by some men as a moral and social blunder and impropriety, and the Word of God has always been acknowledged as declaring it to be a sin. But there was a comparatively recent time when professedly Christian communities were agreed as to the harmlessness and sinlessness of moderate drinking of intoxicants. Discreet exhilaration, unaccompanied by scandal, was winked at. A time came when in the Christian consciousness of some soul was born this new, absolutely new, truth, TO MAKE A BEVERAGE OF THE INTOXICANT IS WRONG. The first disciples of this creed had a hard time of it. They were laughed at as fanatics. They could not get as favorable life insurance rates as moderate drinkers got. The medical profession was almost universally opposed to them. The brewers and distillers, re-enforced by importers and dealers in intoxicants, form the largest business interest of every civilized country; and of course they were all opposed to the new movement. In America and in every country of Europe one of the larger sources of revenue to the state and to the city was derived from the taxation and licensing of wines, beers, and spirits; and of course the financiers of the revenue departments were in a similar position to that in which the silversmiths of Ephesus found themselves on the occasion of Paul's visit. Even to this day total abstinence has made very little progress except among English-speaking peoples. Our French and German cousins tell us, with too much reason to make the telling pleasant, that we needed the new departure very much.

Notable results have been already accomplished. The church as a whole, but not with all its ministers and members, is on the side of total abstinence. Eminent physicians contend that hospitals conducted without the aid of alcoholic stimulants are just as successful as those that use them. Those who hold this opinion are yet in a minority, but the medical profession as a whole are opposed to the drinking customs of society. It is a recognized evil. Every moralist lauds temperance, but the total abstainer asserts that temperance was not very eagerly advocated until total abstinence was advocated. The cry of the more earnest social reformers is that the saloon must go. This question has supplied sociology with much matter for thought. Is it to be license or no license? or if we agree to license this business, shall it be a high or a low license? Shall we adopt local option, or prohibition, or the Gothenburg system? Is drunkenness a disease, and can it be cured? or is it a crime, and ought it to be punished? It is a political question and a church question as well as a social problem.

When we contemplate the number of societies and of organizations that gather round this theme, and when we consider the large place it occupies in political and in social life, it is scarcely possible to believe that in the beginning of this century there was none of it. Then minister and layman indulged in the social glass, and imagined that some stimulant was an essential part of a meal. The tavern-keeper, the distiller, and the brewer might be, and often were, pillars of the church; while keeping a public-house or saloon was as respectable a business as was any other retail trade or handicraft. In the beginning of this century many men who were accounted respectable, and who held high positions in literature and in politics, were deep in their potations and profuse in their profanity. Where and when was the beginning, the first Christian consciousness concerning this evil? We cannot tell. Before all modern movements we find the Abstemii, who could not partake of the cup of the Eucharist on account of their natural aversion to wine. This natural aversion was in the case of the majority a mere physical disgust and repugnance. Indeed, this is beyond a doubt, although in the case of some the abstinence may have been on moral grounds.

Even in that intolerant age would men shrink from making war against a clear case of physical inability. The Calvinists, usually credited with all intolerance, allowed these primitive abstainers to partake of the bread, and merely touch the cup with their lips without swallowing any of its contents: but the Lutherans declared that this tolerance of theirs was neither more nor less than profanation. If we see in this glimpse of church history the generous forbearance of the creed which has been most accused of severity in dogma and in discipline, do we not also see in the action of the Lutherans, not only the outcome of their doctrine of consubstantiation, but also a conviction on their part that the will as well as the physical peculiarity accounted for the conduct of the Abstemii?

The Nazarites of Scripture were abstainers, but their merit consisted in denying themselves in penance and for purification that which it was quite lawful for other men to use. We do not know when and where the first total abstainer on the grounds of morality and conscience lived, but there must have been a first; and when this Christian consciousness came, this truth at once of human and divine origin, a greater revolution began than earth had witnessed since Jesus walked in Palestine, with the exception of the Reformation of religion.

As in the case of slavery, the Bible and the church have been brought into the controversy. Did our Lord make an intoxicating wine? Did he use fermented wine? Does the New Testament teaching lead to the practice of total abstinence on the part of the followers of Jesus? Or is all that we can say, not that we have positively found it in the Bible, but that the Bible does not forbid total abstinence? This revelation of the Christian consciousness is in conformity with the spirit of the Word on this matter of abstinence. This is all that can be said. If this or any other new thing in morals were clearly taught in the Bible, and had never been introduced to earth because we could not see it, although it had been there all the time, we might gain a point in debate by belittling our intelligence; but in point of fact, in this case of total abstinence as a moral and Christian duty, there is as much room for debate as to what the Scriptures really teach as there is in the question of slavery. There is a very important sense in which the Christian consciousness may be regarded as revelation. By this it is not to be understood that it is of equal authority or certainty as is the Word of God, as a rule of life to all men, but it may be of as much authority to the individual. God may teach a man so that his conscience is more outraged by the sin of using strong drink than it is by sins of which specific mention is made, such as frivolity of speech: or he may be more shocked at a man owning slaves than at his being untruthful.

Like every great movement of social reform, this "liquor question," as it is familiarly known, is at once social, religious, and political. The parallel between it and slavery is very suggestive.

(1) Both have come down to us from the earliest dawn of history. Noah's drunkenness led to the prophetic condemnation of Canaan to utter servitude, to be a "servant of servants," or, as it may more forcibly be rendered, "a slave of slaves." One does not know which to condemn most heartily, the shamelessness of

the son or the drunkenness of the father; but all must respect the severe and unsparing simplicity of the narrative.

(2) When the master was excessively cruel, or a man was a noted drunkard, human society disapproved, even when it did not punish.

(3) The Bible declares drunkenness to be a sin, and modifies slavery with merciful and ameliorating provisions.

(4) The Bible does not furnish a conclusive argument against domestic servitude. or against that use of intoxicants which does not reach the stage which we call drunkenness.

(5) The Christian consciousness has pronounced judgment against slavery, and against our social drinking customs.

May we not hope and expect that the comparison may yet be taken one step farther, and we may be able at some future time to add, that the social and convivial drinking customs are as near extinction as is slavery. But if hope dares prophesy for good, may not also experience prophesy for evil? An awful price was paid for the extinction of slavery from civilization. Are the civilized nations of to-day laying up for themselves "wrath against the day of wrath"? Is it to cost blood and tears and toil and national catastrophes to free the slaves of the saloon and of the wine-cup?

Another illustration of the function of the Christian consciousness is supplied by the opium trade. We emphasize the word "trade;" because it is with it, and not with the opium habit, that we have to do. So far as the habit is concerned, much of what we say about drunkenness is applicable to the opium habit. As a trade, or as it has come to be generally known, "the opium trade," is unique. It has no exact parallel. It has been the fashion to make fun of the vessels that sailed from Boston to the African coast freighted with New England rum and with New England missionaries. It was true, too true; but the government of the United States had not treaties with these African despotisms which compelled them to receive the rum. Any chief could issue an order forbidding any of his subjects from buying a drop of the rum; and perhaps if any of these chiefs were to declare the rum-freighted ship a contraband, and clear it out of his port as a public nuisance, the owners of the ship and of the cargo would not get much active sympathy from the government at Washington. No class of men dislike the rum trade more heartily than the missionaries, and we venture to assert that no class of men use less of it than they do. The rum-traders have a manifest advantage in this business, because the African savage in his natural condition is much fonder of rum than he is of missionaries.

The opium trade with China is on an entirely different moral basis. By treaty rights between the government of Her Majesty, the Queen and Empress, China is compelled to receive the opium ships. The Chinese are not compelled to purchase; but their government dare not forbid them to buy, and so they do buy it; for the Chinaman loves opium even better than the African loves rum. Chinamen bewail this importation of the Indian drug, not only because many of them are sufficiently patriotic to bewail the havoc, physical, mental, and moral, which the use of opium is making among the Chinese, but also because there is a native opium business which would "boom," if the expressive slang may be excused, if the article from Hindustan were excluded. Missionaries from England and America, and disinterested

European merchants and travellers, unite in bearing witness to the evils of the opium habit as witnessed in China. From platform, pulpit, and press, this trade is vigorously denounced. It is wrong by the verdict of the Christian consciousness. But, on the other side, there is the Devil's argument that a bargain is a bargain, business is business, and a treaty is a treaty. The agricultural interests of Hindustan must not be sacrificed. East India merchants must not be ruined. We are told by the apologists of this infernal traffic, that the evils of opium have been exaggerated; that if it was not sent from India, it would be sent from somewhere else; and that the Dutch or the French would get the business; or that the stopping of the traffic from India would do no permanent good, for the Chinese would soon raise an inferior, and perhaps a more injurious, opium for themselves.

Meanwhile, the moral and manly fibre of China is strangely weak, as recent events seem to prove; and while it would be a case of special pleading to ascribe the pitiful exhibition that China has made in her war with Japan to the prevalence of the opium habit, who can deny that this baneful drug has had more than a little to do with that nervelessness, dishonesty, incompetence, and cowardice which seem to prevade all ranks and all classes in China.

We call the Christian consciousness in this case "enlightened public sentiment." This is a good phrase. We have no objections to it; but we believe that the torch which enlightens is grasped by the hand of the Christian consciousness. It is interesting as a problem in morals to study the attitude of Christian England in this matter. It may be ventured as an undeniable fact, that from the Empress of India down to the humblest in the empire, there is searching of heart in this matter. How long will it take to shame the government into doing right? It has got to come. When the Christian consciousness is persistently despised, it may become the hammer of God which breaks those who will not bend.

The function of the Christian consciousness is also well illustrated in the attitude of Christendom to gambling. At this point it may be well to anticipate a criticism which may be made, and which can be put very strongly. It may be charged that the Christian consciousness is credited with too much power in social evolution. It may be said that we can imagine the case of a social order in which Christianity is not recognized coming to the conclusion that gambling was injurious to the man or tribe or state. The Indian tribes of North America are notorious and inveterate gamblers. The frequenter of Monte Carlo cannot surpass the Indian in the calmness with which he stakes and loses his last dollar. The Chinaman is also a gambler of the persistent and seemingly incurable type. Missionaries among these peoples have to insist upon their converts abandoning this vice, as being foolish, immoral, and non-Christian. The Archbishop of Canterbury and his clergy, great and small, have a similar task; and if Dame Rumor does not misrepresent the existing condition of social life, they need to begin with those of their own order who think there is nothing wrong in playing whist or any other game for an insignificant stake, merely to give some interest to their evening's amusement.

Our Indian chief, having his own comfort and the good of his tribe at heart, begins to do some serious thinking. He sees that the winners are wasteful, and that the losers, minus their ponies, and even their blankets, are very wretched. Bitter quarrels, which weaken the tribe, too often arise. And so he comes to the conclusion that he will put his foot down on gambling, and will set a good example by himself ceasing to play games of chance for any stake, great or small. In all this there is not even religious consciousness; for his religion, whatever it is, has nothing to do with the matter. Nor, while it improves what may be called the morals of his tribe, is there any moral sense on his part of abstract right and wrong? We may well suppose that our dusky warrior is not troubled with any conscience or ideas or convictions about "the greatest good of the greatest number." He has his own comfort in view, and nothing else. He is a utilitarian, pure and simple. It is evident to him, if he succeeds in suppressing gambling, that in benefiting himself he has benefited others; but though pleased at this, it is not for this that he has undertaken this reform. We may, with certain philosophers, follow the development of the moral idea in this untutored savage. He marks the improvement of tribal affairs with satisfaction. He sees the good that he has accomplished. He is a man, if a savage; and he wonders whether there is not a way in which other crying evils may be suppressed. We are willing to grant all this, but we are not able to produce any instance of the working out of it.

We find a condition of sentiment and of practice among Christian people. It is with this that at present we have to do. Lotteries were once highly respectable. Now they are denied the privileges of the United States Mail. Our Capitol was built in part by lottery schemes, in which the people in general, and the Federalists in particular, had a prominent part. Church fairs in America and bazaars in England were noted and ridiculed for their lottery schemes. The schoolboy risked his marbles, the poor man his coppers, and the rich man his gold, in miscellaneous betting, or in games which might be pure chance, or skill, or a combination of skill and chance. Perhaps this vice was never more rampant than it is in England and America to-day. It has placed its baneful grasp on college sports, on athletic games in general; and the horse-racing of to-day is the saturnalia of the gambler and the bookmaker, who is not only a gambler himself, but a pander to the vices of others. When a rich

American and a prince of England have a yacht-race for five hundred pounds, it is a trifling stake for the deep, well-lined purses of the contestants. It is true that they are not in it for money, but for glory. The paltry stake may be, as it often is, given by the winner to be divided among the crew of the victorious vessel; but the principle of the game of chance is there. The card-party, in which there is no playing for stakes, but where the host and hostess give prizes to the winners, has in it the element of gambling. When we are told that many of the transactions on the stock exchange, the cotton exchange, the corn exchange, and other commercial centres, partake of the nature of gambling — are gambling, pure and simple, we cannot doubt it. When lambs are shorn, and successful corners entail suffering on thousands, and successful bulls or bears push their rivals to the wall, and clean them out as thoroughly as ever Bedouin of the desert despoiled the luckless traveller, or border baron or highland raider cleaned out the castle and cattle-yard of his foe, why should we not with Huxley[1] say, "In my belief the innate qualities, physi-

[1] Evolution and Ethics, p. 13.

cal, intellectual, and moral, of our nation have remained substantially the same for the last four or five centuries," or, as he puts it in the Romanes Lecture of 1893, "If there is a generalization from the facts of human life which has the assent of thoughtful men in every age and country, it is that the violator of ethical rules constantly escapes the punishment which he deserves; that the wicked flourishes like a green bay tree, while the righteous begs his bread; that the sins of the father are visited upon the children; that, in the realm of nature, ignorance is punished just as severely as wilful wrong; and that thousands upon thousands of innocent beings suffer for the crime or the unintentional trespass of one." It may be remarked in passing that these eloquent words state the case very strongly for that future state in which the unredressed wrongs of earth shall be righted, and the everlasting truth shall be vindicated. But while thoughtful men in England and in America justly regard the prevalence of the gambling spirit as being a menace alike to social order and to public virtue, there are signs of promise and tokens of good. The Christian consciousness has been aroused. Legislation has attempted to suppress or to keep in check this growing evil.

It is remarkable how very little there is in the Scriptures bearing directly on this vice. In this respect it is in the same position as is the use of alcoholic drinks or the owning of slaves. Good people gamble in an honorable way, according to their estimate of honor, and they do so to-day, without suspecting themselves of wrong doing. The young ladies who taught in the Sunday-school distinguished themselves by their successful disposing of lottery tickets at the church fair. They sighed and groaned over the heartless Roman soldiers who cast lots for the seamless coat of Christ, the Crucified,[1] and they disposed by lot, fifty cents each, of a handsome set of furs. The prize package, the guess cake, and the New Orleans lottery differ in degree, but not in kind. In many States these things are forbidden to-day by legislation; and in quarters where there is no terror of the law, the church and an ever-growing number of Christian men and women know that the thing which their fathers thought right and proper is wrong — utterly and forever wrong. We do

[1] John xix. 24.

not know where this thought was born, we do not know who was the first to utter the everlasting yea and nay concerning it. The genesis of the new spiritual life in man the *unregenerate* is the same in mode as is the birth of a new truth in man the *regenerate*. "The wind bloweth where it listeth, and thou hearest the sound thereof, but canst not tell whence it cometh, and whither it goeth: so is every one that is born of the Spirit."[1] Gambling is doomed so far as the moral sentiment and the legislation which the Christian consciousness can secure will doom it. The saloon is doomed. It and the gambling-hell must go the way of the slave-mart and the slave-ship. The spiritual forces which are to fight the good fight have been born into the world.

A pleasant story is told of the late Professor Proctor, which, however, we have only by hearsay. At a Boston *conversazione* he was asked by one of Boston's fair and learned daughters, "Professor, what is the law of gravitation?" "Madam," he replied, "the law of gravitation is the will of God." The Christian consciousness in its last analysis is the

[1] John iii. 8.

will of God formulated by men chosen of God.

It need scarcely be said that these three moral and social movements in society and in church life and work are not the only developments in morals that might have been chosen. For example, following a similar train of reasoning, one can study the evolution of the Christian consciousness concerning cruelty to animals, the fighting of animals for sport, pugilism, the duel, and war between nations. Then, there are other great movements which are not yet within the field of the Christian consciousness; but, reasoning from analogy, they will yet find their expounder and their place. In this category we place the relation of labor and capital, the solution of the various forms of social unrest and discontent which find expression in socialism, anarchy, and communism. If we recommended prayer, and a devout waiting for the light of God, as an aid to the solution, many modern philosophers would join hands, or rather, would join voices, with anarchist and socialist in laughing us out of doors. Even United States senators have been found who did not believe in uniting religion with politics. But there was a Christian as well as a free-thinking abolition, and there were Christian slaves as full of trust as of ignorance; but they willed to do the will of God as far as they knew it, when they sang:—

> "'Way down Moses
> 'Way down to Egypt land,
> And tell old Pharaoh
> To let my people go."

It had not the ring of Miriam's song by the Red Sea shore; but it was a cry from the heart. There was and is Christian temperance, and women whom the drink curse has bruised and broken during the centuries are in the van.

There are many honest social reformers filled with the anti-gambling spirit, who are not active Christians, or who may not be Christians at all; but men of faith and prayer are in the forefront of the battle. Spiritual forces have to be accounted for in the development of morals. It is easy to try to turn "Sunday School politics" into ridicule, and it is easy to sneer at Young People's Society of Christian Endeavor reformers; but the future is on their side. It is a simple fact of history, that great moral movements have sometimes been hid from the wise and prudent, and have been revealed unto babes.[1] This was the opinion of Jesus, the Prince of moral and social reformers, those who will not call him Lord being judges.

[1] Matt. xi. 25.

CHAPTER VII

THE ATTITUDE OF THE CHURCH TO EVOLUTION IN MORALS

THE attitude of the church to many of the great moral developments of history is perplexing to many minds. If there is a Christian consciousness, if these new moral births are indeed of divine and human parentage, why should they have received such unaccountable greeting from the church, which professes to be the representative on earth of the divine, the supernatural? The objector of to-day is ready to tell the church and its ministers that they do not come from any unseen holy of special knowledge or power or insight. There is a science, and there is a secularism, which says, "You do not originate anything in morals; true, your Bible has usually fitted the times, but it followed, it did not lead, the grand march; you have never taken the initial steps in any of the great reforms, moral and social; you are never found in the van until observation, experience, and experiment have proven this or that reform to be the coming thing in morals; then, but not till then, you are willing to become its apostles. You do not discover that this new thing is in harmony with your Bible and your creed until by its own merits and its own success it has proved its right to live. The church, the accredited ambassador of heaven, ought to be the first to recognize the heavenly Child; but she is not. These things — and moral truths are things just as much as material substances are — were evolved by a natural process of growth, by the law of their being. When Paul said that things which were seen were not made of things which do appear, he was not only unphilosophical, he was meaningless." Such is the position taken to-day by many eminent men in Europe and America. We find it in newspaper and magazine. It is on the lecture-platform, and has begun to invade the pulpit.

We are told to take the question of slavery as an instance and example. To-day almost all thoughtful men admit that slavery is a moral and social injustice; and injustice is sin against society, even if there be no personal

God against whom, and in whose sight, we can sin. Why did it take so many centuries of Christian culture to find out this truth? How comes it that the expounders of this word of God did not discover the grand truth long ago, and proclaim it from every platform and pulpit and mountain top? Not only was the discovery of this new departure in the life of the world not due to ministers of religion, but after the accursed thing was bravely condemned by the heroic fathers and founders of abolition, ministers of religion denounced them, or took refuge in that neutrality which shelters the coward as well as the sage, or gave but a faint-hearted support until the thing had vindicated its own existence, and demonstrated to the world that it was indeed a moral army on the march, destined to move over the land and over the sea. So says the world; and though the world exaggerates, it is not altogether wrong.

Let a glance be taken at the total abstinence movement. While we may and do differ very much as to the way in which we are to fight this drink curse, it is a growing opinion that the drinking habit, even in moderation, is a moral and social evil. But the world affirms that we have not to thank the church or the Bible for this growing sentiment and public judgment. Only after this thing in morals had vindicated its own existence, and demonstrated to the world that it was one of the coming things in social science, did the church take hold of it, and prove to the world that the Bible was on the side of this new movement. When the air was thick with such charges, need we wonder that they were formulated into such shape as:—

(1) These things which are *now* seen, these great facts in morals, have been made or evolved out of things which do appear; there is no supranatural factor in their evolution; they have no divine parentage.

(2) The church has followed these new movements at a discreet distance, but has never led the van in their promulgation.

These are grave charges; and we have but to read the history of the anti-slavery movement in Britian and in America, and the history of the temperance movement, in order to make frank confession that the charges are not altogether groundless.

There is, however, a great deal to be said in defence of the church:—

(1) The church has been misrepresented, and her backwardness in moral movements has been exaggerated. The church, more especially since the Reformation, has been the warm friend and advocate of all moral movements, even granting that she has been somewhat slow in recognizing the new. In England and in America, the fight for civil liberty was won by virtue derived from the previous training in the struggle for religious freedom. Before the church as a body moves, her individual members have been active in all high enterprises and in all pioneer work; and the men who have been the high priests, and sometimes the martyrs, of social progress, have been, in many cases, devout Christians.[1]

[1] Much of the suffering endured by the early Puritans in England was in the cause of moral and social reform; but these reforms were always exalted into religious tenets. An Oxford man named Prynne, in the beginning of the seventeenth century published a huge unreadable sort of book of one thousand quarto pages, against theatres, dancing, masquerades, and women actors. He did not spare the queen, but had sundry reflections upon her frivolities. To-day she would not be called a specially frivolous woman. He was condemned to expulsion from Oxford and from Lincoln's Inn, fined five thousand pounds, placed in the pillory at Westminster and at

(2) There is a human as well as a divine side to the church. It sometimes happens that her finances and material well-being are in the hands of men not remarkable for personal piety. A church edifice ordinarily represents not only a communion roll, but also a society, trustees, pewholders, etc., who may not all be Christians in the higher sense of that word. Zeal usually welcomes sacrifice, but worldly prudence shrinks from and frowns 1 on this uncomfortable and unmanageable zeal. Need we wonder that the human sometimes impedes the progress of the divine.

(3) The church is a huge body. Denominations are large bodies, and it is the law of such bodies to move slowly. The fiery apostle runs through the world, and is indignant if every sleeper is not awakened by his passing trumpet-blast. His impatience is natural, but nature is sometimes wise and sometimes foolish. Re-

Cheapside. His ears were cut off, his cheeks and forehead branded with hot irons. They burned his offending volume so literally under his nose that he was nearly suffocated with the smoke; and to end all, they imprisoned him for life.

Others were treated with similar cruelty; and his Grace, Archbishop Laud, thanked the lords of the Star Chamber for their just and honorable sentence upon these men, and regretted that he could not resort to more thorough measures.

clining elephants take a much longer time to rise than reclining mice take. The church is an army, not a mob. It is a deliberative assembly even more than it is an army. By the very necessity that is laid upon her to preserve peace within her own borders, and to do no injury to the consciences of her members, a new moral movement may be well under way before the church with harmonious and united ranks can join the grand march of progress.

(4) The church is an aged body; and in social, political, and ecclesiastic affairs, the old are inclined to be conservative. The youngest sect is usually the most radical. Those religious bodies that aspire to be permanently radical, either in dogma or in formula, cannot make much impression upon society. The average man cannot grow old comfortably in a communion that refuses to grow old with him, and comfort is to age what excitement is to youth. There is much current folly about preaching to specific classes and conditions of people. Preach so as to attract the young people, especially the young men. I apprehend that Paul was all things to all men, not

by preaching to young people on courtship, or on the ethics of the Olympian games, or on the morals of the chariot race, but by seizing the common denominator of the spiritual life and by holding it forth — the word of life and of power. Socially the true function of the church is to maintain a certain moral standard, spiritually its true mission is to hold forth the word of life. The same word that comforts age should stimulate youth. The church is a home, not a music hall; a teacher, not a caterer. The church that goes into the dime-show business, and the catering for profit business, reaps present and partial success, and the price that she pays for it is — ultimate failure. In this modern tendency, however, we have simply a reaction from, and rebellion against, the church of history, which has invariably been found at the opposite extreme. The church has very frequently resembled an aged father who instils lofty principles into his children. He himself has made them daring and progressive, and yet he trembles and doubts and fears when they begin to manifest his training of them in some unexpected direction. It is one thing to be conservative, it is quite another thing to boast in the *semper idem*. Every true church is conservative; every false system, in its everlasting certainty concerning itself, claims this attribute of Almighty God — the unchanging.

(5) The prime function of the church is the teaching and nourishing of that enthusiasm for God and for humanity which leavens society with spiritual influences. This is accomplished by the regeneration of individuals as such. The advocacy of any particular item in moral or social reform, though not to be neglected or ignored, is neither her first nor her finest office-work. It is a significant fact, that, though some hideous social abuses, and some disgusting vices which it were shame to name, were common in the days of our Lord, he did not give his apostles special instructions to make a crusade against them. They were to proclaim the coming of the kingdom of God. The light was to chase the darkness. The expulsive power which a supreme affection exercises was to be demonstrated. Moses gave manna. The Christian's manna is everywhere, and Christ gives him leaven. The church is not a knight-errant

running a tilt at this abuse and at that, although she delights in her soldiers doing with their might what their hands find to do. She is an army on the march; and when certain guerillas for good abuse her for not marching with them, she replies, "He that is not against me is for me." She is a sage inculcating the principles that lie at the root of justice and freedom.

Just complaint is also made that the church does not reprove the transgressions of the individual sinner as she should, and as she did in days gone by. We are told that it is an army so voluntary that it can keep together only by relaxing discipline. We admit that the church is a little weak-kneed. The bondage of the pulpit is not all a myth. But it must be admitted that if she is not as wholesomely vigorous as she might be on moral issues, she makes up for it by her keen vigilance on dogmatic issues. In fact, there is a tendency in churches as there is in certain individuals to make up for looseness of life by rigidity of belief. Thirty years ago Scotland had an unhappy notoriety for intemperance and for her statistics of bastardy, and the Southern States had all the moral turpitude which slavery entails; and yet both were orthodox of the orthodox so far as dogma was concerned. But after all the true work of the church is not so much the cultivation of a keen scent for individual heresy and for individual transgression, as it is to rouse the intellect of humanity, to quicken the conscience of humanity, and to renew the heart of humanity.

(6) Every moral movement has its environment. The politician, the economist, and the socialist may all be claiming it or repudiating it. Is it not fair that every such innovation or change should have to struggle into a lusty manhood, and literally prove itself to be a child of God, before the church opens her doors of welcome and of adoption? Almost unconsciously the church has treated principles just as she treats the individuals who seek her fellowship. Men are not received into a church because there is an expectation, or even a probability, that in some future they shall prove to be or will become worthy, good, and true; nor are they usually admitted on a mere verbal confession when there is no knowledge

of their manner of life. They are expected to bear the fruit of the renewed life. The church has treated moral innovations as she has treated men, and this is theoretically fair; but good men and good measures have often received but scant justice at the hands of the church. Our present point of view demonstrates the evenhandedness of her justice, rather than the wisdom of her conduct.

(7) In many countries a union exists between the church and the state. At one time this identification of the church with the state was the rule throughout the whole of Christendom. We do not enter into the merits of such connection. Its warmest advocates will admit that the church and the civil power are not always like-minded. The priest lighted the altar-lamps, but the state treasury supplied the oil; and the church had sometimes to pay a bitter and humiliating price for the support of the state. Even where there is no connection with the state, as in the churches of the United States and in the non-established churches of Britain, moral movements are often related to political parties, and social reforms very often find their way into politics. When

legislation is needed, the political leaders have to be reckoned with, and the action of the church is more or less modified.

These seven considerations take the shape of a cumulative apology; and if to them we add the timidity, lukewarmness, and unfaithfulness to which the churches like individuals, must plead guilty, the wonder is, not that the church has done so little, but that it has done so much, as a pioneer in ethics and morals.

When we have said all that can be said in apology for the church's relation to the evotluion of morals, we feel that there is an unexplained remainder; and this consists in the church's denying of, or ignorance of, the Christian consciousness. She has known the truth that comes by theological science, by interpretation of Scripture, and by the logic of events, and the truth has made her free as far as her knowledge fitted her for freedom; but her Christian consciousness has been to a great extent allowed to lie dormant. When it has been discussed at all, it has been put aside with a certain shrinking timidity, which seems to say, "Do not let us have anything to do with it. If we once open our doors to its official recognition, we shall be overwhelmed with a whole army of cranks and of enthusiasts, and we shall be forced out of our own well-worn grooves." Let us beware of treating with neglect or with contempt the man who comes before the church or the world with a new thought concerning life and progress; for this man or woman may be the God-appointed instrument through whom a new idea, a moral truth, is to be born into the world.

Sometimes the churches have been eager to rush into the opposite extreme. Some churches in the United States made abolition principles a *sine qua non* of membership, some to-day make total abstinence a condition, and others non-membership of secret societies. In certain communions there is a tendency to increase rather than to diminish such tests. The error of such a course, the narrowness and unwisdom of it, are apparent. It is granted that a church must have such unity in its dogmatic and ethical standards as will enable its members to feel that they are brethren living together in unity, but there should be room for the full play of of individuality in faith and in practice. The church is not made strong by dabbling in ethics, letting down these bars and putting up those. To-day a member is disciplined because he dances, but unrebuked he takes his wine. To-morrow the dancing is ignored, and the strong drink is condemned. To-day we cannot see how a Christian can consistently go to the theatre, but there is no harm in his belonging to a secret oath-bound society; but to-morrow we feel kindly toward the theatricals, especially if amateur and devoid of artistic merit, and we pronounce anathema upon the member of the secret society.

We can suppose the case of a man who is a believer, sound on the cardinal doctrines and of exemplary life, save for this opinion that he holds, and which he is man enough to avow. You will not let him into your church. If you are right, you should rejoice if every church followed your example. This child of God becomes a pariah, a religious outcast, with no Lord's Table where he is welcome, with none that he can call his own. In this way very ordinary sorts of men have been converted into martyrs and heroes, and enriched with all the bitter-sweet satisfaction that comes from a chronic sense of injustice. Coercion in non-essentials hinders the cause it seeks to help, and a church should exercise great care before it makes belief in or participation in any moral movement an essential. The sumptuary legislation in which both church and state delighted in the past is no longer possible, but a good deal of social tyranny in the name of zeal for morals and manners is still possible. One of the glories of the church ought to consist in its being the place where really good men can forget a hundred differences because of their supreme oneness in Christ.

You may make rules to the effect that no member of your church shall be permitted to dance, or use strong drink as a beverage, or be a member of a secret society, or play cards in any shape or manner. Suppose that each one of those practices is more or less reprehensible. You have got a clean and rather unique society from an ethical point of view; but lo! you have converted your church into a club, and your Lord's Table has become an exclusive feast for those whose own worthiness is the measure of their neighbors' unworthiness.

There is an evolution in morals subject to

the creative acts of God. This evolution the church recognizes and guides, but does not always lead. It advocates without invariably assuming the right to enforce. It works without assailing the liberties of the individual. It is not pledged to teach any physical science or any mechanical art, but it is pledged to teach a pure ethic to society as such, and to teach the art of holy living and peaceful dying to the individual as such. In doing this its trust is in God, its charter is the word of Revelation. In the daily struggle onward and upward, it knows a superintending, inspiring, and creating God. The Christian consciousness is its hill of vision, and its watchword is, "Things which are seen were not made of things which do appear."

CHAPTER VIII

THE RELIGIOUS CONSCIOUSNESS OF THE HEATHEN

THE question is often asked as to how we can explain the elevation of moral sentiment, and the religious consciousness, which are found in some of the so-called heathen writers. When the sayings of Socrates, Plato, Marcus Aurelius, and others are quoted, we speak of their guesses at truth, or of their inspiration, or of their familiarity with the Hebrew Scriptures, or with the Hebrew theology as expounded by masters in Israel. We claim that our view of the Christian consciousness is not radically affected or influenced by the views that may be held with regard to the religious consciousness in general. This makes it unnecessary to enter upon any minute consideration of the relation between inspiration and the heathen cults. Moreover, this is a subject on which much has been said, and there is an abundance of material for study, though a good deal of it is of a fragmentary description. But on the other hand, the very abundance of reference, and the many uses to which it has been put, call for a brief review of the outstanding facts in the case.

Geology, the Book of Genesis, the Nineveh tablets, and the almost universal tradition of nations, bear testimony to the fact of the Deluge. We assume the genuineness and authenticity of the Mosaic account of the Flood. The closing paragraph of Sir William Dawson's latest work, "The Meeting-place of Geology and History," states the case so admirably that we quote it in full. "We have merely glanced cursorily at a few of the salient points of the relation of the primitive history of man in Genesis to modern scientific discovery. Many other details might have been adduced as tending to show similar coincidences of these two distinct lines of evidence. Enough has, however, been said to indicate the remarkable manner in which the history in Genesis has anticipated modern discovery, and to show that this ancient book is in every way trustworthy, and as remote as possible from the myths and legends of ancient heathenism; while it shows the historical origin of beliefs which, in more or less corrupted forms, lie at the foundations of the oldest religions of the Gentiles, and find their true significance in that of the Hebrews. To the Christian, the record in Genesis has a still higher value, as constituting those historical groundworks of the plan of salvation, to which our Lord himself so often referred, and on which he founded so much of his teaching."

We are in the best of scientific company and fellowship when we make the Flood a historic starting-point, but one who believes in and writes about the Christian consciousness must be entitled to assume the credibility of the Old Testament record. Noah and his immediate descendants possessed the knowledge of the true God. Apart altogether from any supernatural element entering into its preservation, from that continuity of forms which ritual gives, and from that persistence of doctrine which faith begets, it is simply impossible to conceive of this knowledge of God and worship of him coming to a sudden or abrupt termination. Error dies hard, and there is a sense in which truth never dies. It is obscured, almost blotted out; but there is enough of the stately edifice left to guide the architect in its restoration. The Bible is very silent as to the period of over four hundred years which elapsed between Noah and the call of Abraham. The incident of Babel, brief notes of the dispersions after the Flood and after Babel, and the genealogies of the sons of Noah, are all, about four minutes of reading-matter for four centuries. The worship of the true God did not flee the earth entirely, but it was sadly distorted by the inventions of mankind. It seems as if, when men, by reason of the growing mists of ignorance, error, and superstition, were no longer able to look into the home of God, at heaven's gates they found the objects of their adoration; and so it comes to pass that sun and moon and stars are among the earliest objects of worship. It is easier to believe in and to follow the descent from pure theism to this worship of the powers of nature, to this converting of the worthy dead into demi-gods, the unworthy into dismal shades, to the worship of the reproductive principle and power, or of beauty, or of law and order, than it is to believe in the evolution of the native New Zealander or the inhabitants of the South Sea Islands up to monotheism. History tells us of nations that have retrograded in morals and in worship, but there is no record of any nation rising without help from without. The most intellectual race of the historic past thanks Cadmus for its alphabet, the British Druids get the fire of the new life from a Latin missionary. The virile races of Northern Europe completed that Fall of Rome which internal corruption made an easy task, but Christian Rome conquered her captors. So it has always been. We can believe in the unaided growing worse; but when from the lowest depths we are to be lifted, help must come from without. This is the history of the beginnings of civilization.

Terah, the father of Abraham, went part of the way from Mesopotamia, and in Genesis the initiative in the movement is ascribed to him as the head of the clan; but Moses, Nehemiah, and Stephen, all unite in declaring that Abraham went to Canaan after his father's death in Haran in obedience to the divine voice. We have a hint that his family had to a certain extent fallen away from purity of worship before this call, but it does not seem to surprise Abraham that God should reveal himself. He knows God, and we have no reason to suppose that he was the only one on earth who knew the only one and true God. The journey from Mesopotamia to Palestine was, comparatively speaking, a much longer journey then than it is now; but at the extreme end of it Abraham encounters Melchizedek, King of Salem and priest of the Most High God. Abraham was the priest as well as the chief of his clan, but Melchizedek blesses him. Without entering into any of the discussion which has gathered round this most mysterious personage of Scripture, it will be granted that he was the priest of the true God. The generally received interpretations of the Book of Job are at one in agreeing that it bears testimony to the fact that this ancient patriarch was a prominent figure among other believers who were called the sons of God. We have no reason for supposing that Jethro was the priest of a purely heathen cult. In the incident of Balaam and Balak we have a disobedient prophet; but there is not the slightest reason for supposing that he was not a veritable prophet of God, knowing him, and believing in him. Nor need we think the less of him as a patriot and as a man, if he would fain have cursed this people on the march, in whom he saw the foes of his own people, and perhaps their future destruction. If the Magi were Jews of the dispersion, we can understand their intelligent thoughts concerning the expected Messiah; but if they were representations of the Gentile world, is it not reasonable to suppose that they represented the men of faith and prayer who had not lost their knowledge of God?

It is too common to put the case as if it were a question as to whether the ancient world, and notably the sages of Greece, got their knowledge in part from intercourse with the Hebrew nation and contact with Hebrew thought, or is all that they accomplished the result of intellectual and ethical evolution? But the real question is as to how much of the traditional and inherited knowledge of God we may reasonably suppose them to have possessed. If it can be demonstrated that in addition to the possession of this lingering remnant of the knowledge of God, we can add the almost certainty of their knowledge of contemporary Jewish thought and writings, the case is strengthened, not only by the existence of another source of knowledge, but also by the fact that this second kind, that from contact with the Hebrew, comes to minds that are to a certain extent prepared for it by their first source of knowledge of the truth.

What reason have we to suppose that the Hebrew thought had its influence upon the rest of the world, and that the thought of the Gentile world had more or less influence upon the Jews? The Septuagint is evidently the work of translators of unequal ability, and it is quite likely that it was not all produced at one time; but there is little doubt that it was in the possession of the Alexandrian Jews two hundred and fifty years before Christ. The Jews in many cases were doubtless unable to read their Hebrew Scriptures, hence this version. But whatever were the reasons for making this Greek version, it is difficult to conceive of its existence in a great centre of Greek literary activity, and yet escaping the notice of the acute and inquiring Greek mind. In the days of David and Solomon the land of Israel occupied a prominent place among the teeming population that was in continual flux on the eastern shores of the Mediterranean. When civilization centred in the Euphrates Valley, we know from the Books of Ezra, Nehemiah, Daniel, and Esther, that the Jews sometimes were prominent in the state, and their religious practices and tenets must have been more or less familiar to the peoples among whom they dwelt. In the early Christian church, Seneca was claimed by some as a Christian. Many of his thoughts resemble the Apostle Paul's; and it does not concern our position whether Seneca was indebted to Paul, or whether the great apostle of the Gentiles was indebted to the illustrious Roman. Nor does it matter whether or not we regard the resemblances as being simply the results of similar training on the part of men of germane intellectual habit. Mr. Huxley tells us with evident satisfaction that "There are a good many people who think it obvious that Christianity also inherited a good deal from Paganism and from Judaism; and that if the Stoics and the Jews revoked their bequests, the moral property of Christianity would realize very little." To do Mr. Huxley justice, it must be admitted that in other parts of his versatile authorship he has spoken more appreciatingly of the "moral property of Christianity." The Christian scholar regards the New Testament as a growth from the Old. The founder of Christianity said that he did not come to destroy the law, but to fulfil it. As to the morals which we have got from the philosophers of Greece, we need not inquire as to the bulk or the quality of them. The question at issue is, Where did these philosophers themselves get their morals, which the New Testament adopts and indorses? Justin Martyr recognizes the worth of much of the Pagan philosophy, and he attributes it to the "*logos*" which was always in the world. We do not know, at this day, the sources of information possessed by Clement of Alexandria, but his opinion is entitled to respect; and he tells us that Plato had the Bible, and that Homer was indebted to it. It is quite within the range of guarded imagination to conceive of a good deal of intercourse between merchants and dignitaries of Israel and the other peoples of the Levant in those days when the wonderful Temple was in course of erection, and the wealth and glory of Solomon were attracting attention on every side. The meeting-place was Phœnicia, famous alike for its commerce, culture, and skill in handicraft. In passing, it is to be noted that these statements of Justin Martyr's and Clement's will not fit very well into the "Higher Criticism" of to-day, because, according to it, there was little or no Bible in the time of Plato, and scarcely any in the days of Homer.

If to the knowledge of God which came down from the dawn of history, the precious, but too easily forgotten, knowledge which the descendants of Noah possessed, we add the knowledge that came from contact with Hebrews, and with their literature, is there not a strong case for the possession by some of a religious consciousness which was not wholly the product of evolution? Our argument is historical, not doctrinal; nor is it desirable at this stage to introduce such an argument, but from the Christian standpoint, it is evidently legitimate to add whatever of illumination there came to the men of the pre-Christian era from the eternal *logos*.[1] He was "the true light which

---

[1] The idea of the Resurrection was held by Democritus, and was scoffingly referred to by Pliny. Lucretius almost

lighteth every man that cometh into the world."[1] Every man has a part, much or little, of that light. This was something more

quotes Ecclesiastes. Homer gave the soul wings by which it flew out of the body into the mansions of the dead.

This brief editorial from the Boston *Congregationalist* of the 28th of February, 1895, is significant: —

DO ALL HAVE EQUAL SPIRITUAL OPPORTUNITIES?

No and yes. The child of a Pagan African Bushman certainly cannot be said to have an equal opportunity to acquire spiritual knowledge with the child of an enlightened, consecrated New England or Ohio household. The one knows next to nothing about God, and nothing at all about Jesus Christ or revealed truth. The other has inherited the Christian riches of the centuries, and understands not only his opportunities of religious growth, but also his responsibility for their use. A wider contrast than that between two such children hardly can be imagined. The one certainly is not upon an equal footing in the matter with the other.

But they may be regarded from another point of view. Suppose the soul of the African child, as childhood develops into maturity, to feel a precious consciousness of the presence of the great God, to strive feebly yet earnestly to obey and please him, and to be devoted, however imperfectly, to the effort to live loyally up to the little spiritual light which has been afforded. Suppose the American child to be, as so many, alas! are, often indifferent, rather than increasingly devoted, to God, and to grow in holiness only sluggishly and by no means as fast or as far as possible.

Now, although the latter may attain a moral plane far higher than that of the former, and even may have started upon a plane much higher than the highest ever attained by the former, it may be the young African, not the American, who at last has risen more from his original state toward God, who has made the longer progress toward holiness, who has exhibited the more genuine spiritual earnestness and fidelity. And this may be, and doubtless is, what God values most. So that in respect to the possibility of spiritual progress, which is the essential matter, the two cases supposed, and all cases, stand upon the sam footing. Each has been granted an equal opportunity to rise. How else, indeed, could God be fair, as he must be?

[1] John i. 9.

than the mere light of nature. Our plea for the possession of the religious consciousness other and more than natural evolution can give, is a threefold cord.

At this point it may be argued that the religious consciousness does not leave much more for the Christian consciousness to confer on those who possess it. Saul of Tarsus was a man able to judge in this matter. So far as we can judge, his religious consciousness was developed before his conversion to Christianity. He was not lacking in moral earnestness. Now, it so happens that Paul the Christian throws out a singular and altogether remarkable challenge to history bearing on this matter. He says: "For seeing that in the wisdom of God the world through its wisdom knew not God, it was God's good pleasure through the foolishness of the preaching to save them that believe." [1] This is the culmination of an eloquent strain of rejoicing in the power of Christ's death. The world was in — had sunk into — a position which is plainly described as not knowing God. This evidently had not always been the case. The world had come to this

[1] Cor. i. 21.

ignorance of God in, by, or through its wisdom. This was God's decree. It was in the wisdom, will, and plan of God. It is only a halting logic which limits the Eternal Omniscient. With Omnipotence on the one hand, and the freedom of the human will on the other; it is not reason, but imagination, conjecture, and hypothesis, which tries to reconcile and explain this coexistence. When man's wisdom failed, then God's plan of salvation, his means to that end, was to come into play. It was the foolishness or simplicity of preaching.

Without entering upon any discussion of the literature that has gathered round questions as to the date of the authorship of the historical books of the Old Testament, it is to be noted that, by almost common consent, the long line of the prophets came to a close about four hundred years before Christ, and then came the centuries of God's silence. The world was left to its own wisdom; and never had the wisdom of the world a better chance to excel than in those centuries. They were ushered in by Socrates, who was persuaded about the reality of his religious mission, and who believed in the divine voice that spoke to him. He taught the doctrine of contented poverty by precept and by example. He was the greatest ethical teacher that the world has ever seen. Plato, his pupil, was the master of dialogue and of philosophy. Both were profound moralists. The roll-call of the century which was heralded by these greatest of the Greeks, say from 400 to 300 B.C.. is unequalled in history. Aristotle, philosopher, logician, and mathematician; Diogenes the Cynic, the keenest of critics; Euclid, geometrician and philosopher; Zeno, father of the Stoics; and Epicurus of the Epicureans, — were all men of this marvellous century. Nor were the gentler elements of life lacking. From Homer, Herodotus, Xenophon, and Phidias, they had a rich inheritance of poetry and art. It was the age, not only of philosophy, but also of poetry, art, and oratory. Rome conquered Greece by arms, and Greece conquered Rome by her philosophy. These centuries witnessed not only the glory of Roman power, but also her Augustan age of literature.

The civilization of the West was only that of one-half of the world. Another half lay to the east of this singular people who dwelt in Palestine. There we find Buddhism. It is the fashion amongst certain visionaries and extremists in these days to find wonderful comfort in Buddha. The world is indebted to Max Müller, Rhys Davids, and other Oriental students for the light that they have thrown upon that system of belief which influences more or less the destinies of four hundred millions of our fellow beings. But there are others who are visionaries when they are not frauds, and who are not philosophers in either case, who find what seems to be sometimes a morbid and sometimes an ecstatic satisfaction in certain occult mysteries and puerile miracles. Every man lives by faith. We must believe, even if our faith is a belief in unbelief. The devotees of Western spiritualism and of Eastern occultism are cousins-german.

David Hume was a bachelor; and he lived with his mother, a good old Scotch lady, who was not troubled with her famous son's scepticism. Nor does she seem to have been much troubled about him. This pleasant story is told of her. It is one of those stories which ought to be true if it is not, — a story which is a parable if it is not history. She was entertaining certain old ladies of Edinburgh to tea;

and with engaging frankness of sympathetic intimacy, one of them remarked: "It must be hard for you, Mrs. Hume, to live with a man like your son David, who believes in nothing." "My son David believe in nothing!" retorted the old lady. "It's little ye ken about my Dauvit. He'll believe anything that is not in the Bible."

Edwin Arnold gives the date of Buddha as B.C. 623. Max Müller places it at B.C. 557. But Rhys Davids, perhaps the first authority on this question, gives the date as B.C. 492. He belonged to the same generation as Phidias and Socrates. The best thought of India came just before the divine silence began. In China, Confucianism assumed its present form about B.C. 500; and Lao-tse, the founder of Taoism, was the contemporary of Socrates and of Buddha. Did ever the world have such a chance as it had in these four centuries that preceded the Christian era? East and West there was phenomenal intellectual activity, æsthetic culture, artistic skill, and literary activity. Nor was there lacking, seemingly, the moral and spiritual capital which are required for the higher business of the world. Contact with the Jew remained; but the knowledge of God that once filled the earth was a rapidly vanishing possession. The wisdom of the world was having its opportunity and trial. So Paul says. Even the man who does not believe in the inspiration of the Scriptures has, as a mere matter of literary criticism, to accept the genuineness and authenticity of Paul's letters. His inspiration may be denied, but his work cannot be ignored. He tells us that the wisdom of the world was on its trial; and the result was that this wisdom, whatever else it did, blotted out the knowledge of God. "The world through its wisdom knew not God."

Let us suppose that some student of moral and social problems flourished B. C. 300. All the mighty men whom we have named have passed away; but almost all of them are men of the last hundred and fifty years. Our student watches the throbbing, earnest, quickened life of Greece, and, patriot as he is, dreams fondly of the good time coming from it all. Nor can he help rejoicing for humanity's sake in the vigorous and virtuous Roman Republic, even though he fears while he admires. While this is the state of his mind and of his knowledge, an adventurous Greek comes to Athens from far-off India. He tells our sage the story of the great Indian reformer. He gives rose-colored but fair information as to what has already been accomplished, and as to what the hope of India is. And yet another comes bearing tidings from afar. He has been to far-off Cathay and beyond, and has a strange story to tell of a civilization which is young and hopeful, of a great philosopher, and of a great reformer. The thoughtful Greek hears their wonderful stories, and rejoices. Is there not good reason to believe that the world is on the eve of mighty changes for good? Why should he not grow prophetic in his zeal, and believe in the coming good and in the coming wisdom? What did come of it all? — of these centuries of philosophy, poetry, and art, which were also centuries throbbing with new spiritual impulses, with the vigor of new creeds, and with the enthusiasm of new leaders? Let the first chapter of Romans answer the question. Let Gibbon bear his testimony all unswayed by zeal for the Christian faith. Read Farrar's " Early Days of Christianity." All authorities unite in telling a somewhat similar shameful story. The wisdom of the world was a dismal failure. Insincerity, cruelty, and selfishness were rampant. Society was honeycombed with vice. The anticipations of the sage had not been fulfilled. The world had grown worse.

The pleasant city of Pompeii lies beside the great mountain. It is not a capital like Rome, having the wealth, gayety, and vices of an imperial centre. It is a fair representative of the average prosperous community of that day. It was buried, as one might say, instantaneously, and it lay buried for long centuries. The excavation of the buried city tells us just how they lived when our Lord walked this earth. It is a sad story of artistic excellence and of moral filth. Christ came in the fulness of time, so far as earth's need of some one to show it goodness, truth, and life was concerned. The Christian consciousness came into a world from which the religious consciousness had almost vanished, so far as any knowledge of the true God, any pure theism, was concerned. History tells of the decline and fall, as well as of the evolution and ascent, of nations and of individuals. When the centuries of the divine silence began, the world had a good amount of moral and spiritual capital; but her wisdom proved to have a fatal defect. She lost almost all her capital, and Jesus came into a world that was morally and spiritually bankrupt.

CHAPTER IX

THE RELATION OF THE CHRISTIAN CONSCIOUSNESS TO DOCTRINE

In considering the relation of the Christian consciousness to development or evolution of doctrine, we are met first of all by those who deny that there is any such thing as an evolution or development of doctrine. Fortunately, however, this is not a question of theory, but of fact; and to the facts in the case we propose to appeal. We have also to encounter the difficulty of discriminating between moral sanctions and dogmatic statements. For example, the Southern preachers declared that abolition was an atheistical principle; and the abolitionists of the North, who were in sympathy with religion, in many cases desired a church in which the holding of sound abolition principles would be a test of membership. The issue was transferred from morals to doctrine by both parties. In the temperance question, when a church takes official action in favor of prohibition, it not only asserts a dogma, or doctrine of the church, but it also lifts the question into the arena of practical politics. To this it may be replied that this is not one of the great doctrines of theology. True, it has not a history, because it is new. It does not require an apologetic literature, because there has not been division on account of it, or much organized attack of it; but it is doctrine, nevertheless, and of more practical importance to-day, and more of a living issue in Protestantism to-day, than is, let us say, baptismal regeneration, or the difference between consubstantiation and transubstantiation.

Much depends upon our definition of doctrine. Is it the thing taught? Then the word embraces the whole of revelation. Is it that which is necessary for salvation? Then it covers a few simple truths. Is it those truths that are commonly held in all the churches? Then many doctrines will be excluded. Is it the confessional symbols of each denomination and the sum total of all of them? Then the field is very wide. There is a sense in which we may claim that every moral movement is related to some phase of Christian doctrine, and it is equally true that every doctrine will have moral issues; but it is easily understood and readily accepted when we say that the thought of the church about the use of alcoholic drinks is a moral problem, and her thought about the salvation of the heathen is a question in doctrine.

In choosing the doctrine of the salvation of infants as affording our first illustration of the relation of the Christian consciousness to development in doctrine, let it be steadily kept in mind that the question before us is not as to the truth of the doctrine, or the opposite, but simply a question as to the *how*, — the mode by which the present largely prevailing opinion came into the church. What was the prevalent opinion on this question after the Reformation? It goes without saying that those churches which believe in baptismal regeneration do not believe in the salvation of all infants. It is well known that infant salvation was not taught in the Calvinistic churches of the seventeenth century. Their creeds do not teach it, and much of their literature proves that the opposite opinion was held. It was never asserted that all infants were lost, but it was plainly taught that many fell short of salvation. Some of these churches held that baptism signified and sealed the partaking of the benefits of the covenant of grace, but only the children of members of the church could be baptized. Another church said there is no salvation without baptism, but we will baptize every child. And yet another said baptism is the privilege and duty of believers; therefore we will not baptize any man until he is able in years, in knowledge, and in heart to make confession of his own faith. The elect infants were the unconscious heirs of grace. Calvin's position about the chosen children, is in this sentence, " *Quos parvulos Dominus ex hac vita recolligit, non dubito regenerari arcana Spiritus operatione.*" To-day the salvation of infants is very generally believed throughout Protestant Christendom. No doubt a very good argument can be made in favor of this belief. It may be briefly outlined as follows: granting that a clean thing cannot come out of an unclean, granting original sin and the guilt of it, in what sense did Christ taste death for this infant, if it was not to wash away this inherited stain?[1] He is the Saviour of all men, especially of those that believe.[2] If a child grows and be-

---

[1] Heb. ii. 9.   [2] 1 Tim. iv. 10.

lieves he is saved; surely if he dies before he can choose between good and evil he will not be lost. Jesus said, " Of such is the kingdom of God." [1] Therefore the children are the sons of God. They either do not need to be born again, or they have been born again. In either case, " He is the propitiation for our sins: and not for ours only, but also for the sins of the whole world." [2] According to such a view of the truth, the child should be taught that he is the child of God, and will be his child forever, unless by his own act he goes into the far country of sin and disobedience. He should not be taught that he is a hell-deserving little wretch. If such views are right, do we not need to reconstruct our theology concerning baptism? God's ordinances are for God's people. Do we not baptize the child and the adult for the same reason, because of their being children of God, saved by his grace? This more hopeful creed and sunnier theology may be true or it may not. These sixteenth and seventeenth century divines were better theologians than we are. There is an inexorable chain of reasoning in favor of their views. The world's thought on

[1] Mark x. 14. [2] 1 John ii. 2.

this subject has not changed by a logical process, but the Christian consciousness has asserted itself. It says, "Your logic may be faultless, and your interpretation may be correct; but it is not the will of God, it is not the thought of God. The time will surely come when the error in your logic and in your interpretation will be clear to all the world. Meanwhile, the position of my Christian consciousness is not that I will not believe, but that I cannot believe as you do." Does not this describe the attitude of many?

There is a good deal of indefinite writing and speaking in these days about the *Zeit Geist*, the spirit of the age. It is regarded as explaining a condition of things, whereas it is merely the putting of a label upon it. The spirit of the age is the consensus of opinion. Some men may hold an opinion almost in spite of themselves, and with a certain amount of mental reservation and unwillingness; some entertain it very doubtingly and tentatively; and some are its confident and enthusiastic promulgators. In secular affairs the spirit of the age is the aggregate consciousness of a community; in morals and doctrine it is the Christian consciousness.

We are sometimes told by a certain class of apologists that the sixteenth and seventeenth century men were so busy with their fight with Rome and with the necessary formulation of their systematic theology, that they had no time for the consideration of those ethical, moral, and even dogmatic issues that are of so much interest to us. But as a matter of fact, they had both time and inclination to reduce their theories to practice; and the moralities were looked after with all the vigilance to be expected of a dominant church which had freed itself spiritually from Rome, but had not freed itself from the traditional policy of Rome. The question as to whether the seventeenth or the nineteenth century belief concerning the salvation of infants is the correct interpretation, applies not only to this doctrine, but to every doctrine that has been modified by the Christian consciousness.

THE SALVATION OF THE HEATHEN.

This question has been so much and so keenly debated of late years that it is not necessary for our purpose in this work to go into it. The trial of a professor of Andover

Theological Seminary, and the prolonged discussion in the American Board, as to its relation to those candidates for the mission field who entertained the larger hope of the possibility of salvation after death, by the presentation of the Christ, whom in life they had no opportunity of knowing, and therefore no opportunity to accept or to reject, has brought this doctrine very prominently before the public mind. But it has been not altogether as friendly to the acceptance of belief in the salvation of the heathen as might be supposed, because it, as it were, prescribed the one method by which it was secured. This "one chance more" doctrine is rejected by many who entertain a hope of the salvation of some of the heathen. In the preceding chapter we have endeavored to state the considerations which may be regarded as justifying the Christian consciousness for this belief concerning the future of, not all the heathen. But the Christian consciousness, while it needs rational sanctions, does not always wait for exegetical justification; and just in this must always lie its strength and its weakness. What is the difference between a rational sanction and a theological justification? It may be put in this way. If to whom much is given, of him much shall be required; and to whom little is given, little shall be required; it follows that to whom nothing is given, nothing shall be required. The use or the abuse of the knowledge given, therefore, seals the fate of man. The abstract conception of supreme justice enables us to believe in the impossibility of any going away from the throne of the Eternal Justice feeling or believing that they have been hardly dealt with. Therefore the heathen who makes shipwreck of life must feel not only that he is reaping as he sowed, but also that he had light enough to sow in other fashion, had his free will so chosen and consented. This may be called a rational sanction for the Christian consciousness; but it will not satisfy it, neither will it create it. The thought of God, and the witness of God, are there.

An exegetical or theological justification is another thing; and here, again, the seventeenth century theologian has the victory. He can and does prove that the heathen are perishing almost if not altogether without exception.

He not only proved it; he believed it. And yet for a century and a half he made no effort to reach them, no effort to obey the last command of his risen Lord. Even dignitaries of the Church of England made fun of the beginnings of missionary work in India. They now believe it; and in every Protestant country under heaven you will find towns or hamlets of say from three hundred to one thousand inhabitants with about two or three times the clerical force necessary for their best, highest good; and Ethiopia in vain stretches out her hands unto God, and there is not one worker for a hundred thousand of those who are perishing.

Is it to be wondered at if the Christian consciousness testifies thus to itself: "Ah, no! the church does not believe. She only thinks she believes it. Would the church wrangle over vestments, and wax candles, and ecclesiastical tailoring? Would she waste her energies over questions pertaining to the province of reverent and scholarly specialists? Would she expend so much energy as she does now in a hundred ways if she really and truly believed that the perishing millions were sinking into perdition, and over the very edge of the pit were waiting in vain for life. Ah, no! the church does not believe; she only thinks she believes." It would be easy to prove that this soliloquy of the Christian consciousness was all wrong because so utterly out of historical perspective, and conceding so little to the imperfection of human nature, and to the unfaithfulness of Christians; but then you do not succeed in convincing the Christian consciousness. Nay, more, this stubborn Christian consciousness declares: "I know God; your theology is wrong. I may not be able to prove it, but it is erroneous; and the time is coming when it will not be taught in your schools; and then for Christ's sake you will do more for the heathen than you are doing now." The appeal is to the verdict of time; and let it go to its chosen time and place of decision. There is neither pleasure nor profit in debating it now. But it is well to keep in mind the outstanding facts of the case.

There are certain features common to the doctrines of infant salvation, and the salvation of the heathen.

(1) As a rule the churches of the Reforma-

tion did not believe in, and did not teach, the salvation of infants or of the heathen.

(2) Their condemnation was not only believed in; it was the theme of discourses in the pulpit, and found its place in the popular literature[1] and verse of the period.

---

[1] Michael Wigglesworth was the most wretched rhymster who ever achieved a reputation, even in those colonial days of New England of which Prof. Coit Tyler says: "Neither advanced age, nor high office, nor mental unfitness, nor previous respectability, were sufficient to protect any one from the poetic vice." His "Day of Doom" was the most popular and widely read book in America previous to the Revolution. This is his picture of the wicked at God's Judgment Bar.

> "With dismal chains and strongest reins
>   Like prisoners of hell,
> They're held in place before Christ's face,
>   Till He their doom shall tell.
> These void of tears, but filled with fears,
>   And dreadful expectations;
> Of endless pains, and scalding flames,
>   Stand waiting for damnation."

Wigglesworth put into execrable verse what the preachers of his day taught in ornate but forcible prose. It was an overconfident theology. It knew everything.

The Puritan divines were as infallible in their way as Rome was. In the seventeenth century every man was a dogmatist of the severest type, until with the end of the century came the inevitable reaction. But to return to Wigglesworth. He proceeds to parade his theology in reply to those who had died in infancy, and who pleaded that they had never done good or evil personally, but had been straightway carried "from the womb into the tomb."

(3) Theoretically and officially the churches have not changed their doctrinal position with regard to these two doctrines.

(4) There has, however, been a change in the thought and feeling of the churches; and this change has been manifested by demands for simpler and shorter creeds, and for modified forms of subscription to existing creeds.

> "You sinners are; and such a share
>   As sinners may expect,
> Such you shall have, for I do save
>   None but mine own elect.
> Yet, to compare your sins with their
>   Who lived a longer time,
> I do confess, yours is much less,
>   Though every sin's a crime.
> A crime it is, therefore, in bliss
>   You may not hope to dwell;
> But unto you, I shall allow
>   The easiest room in hell."

Can a dismal anthropomorphism go any farther? Wigglesworth's God is a sort of gloomy and glorified Oliver Cromwell. But Wigglesworth's God was the God of the Protestant majority in Britain and in America. Need it be added that Roman Catholics and Sacramentarians in the Episcopal Church and in other communions taught the hopelessness of the case of those who died unbaptized. The former view has changed; the latter has not. The former view said, "The guilt of the parent is upon the child;" the latter view said, "The act of faith and duty on the part of the parent and of the church has saved the child."

In the debates of the famous Westminster Assembly, there was substantial agreement as to doctrine, but there was great difference as to government.

(5) These doctrines are not preached as they were in former years. There is either a significant silence, or a bold proclamation of faith in the future wellbeing and blessedness of the children.

(6) The change of view has been so far much more marked and decided in the case of the salvation of infants than in that of the salvation of the heathen.

If our doctrinal or theoretic position has not changed, we naturally expect to find the cause of this change of belief in our modified conceptions of the character of God, as revealed to us by and in our Christian consciousness. We cannot lay too much emphasis upon the modifications of doctrine that come from changing and larger and juster conceptions of the character of God, for this is peculiarly the finest office work of the Christian consciousness. There are doctrinal changes and differences in which the character of God is not involved; or, rather, let us put it as changes in which our ethical and moral conceptions of the divine character are not involved. For example, the questions as between pre- and post-millenarian views are always interesting, and were never more interesting than at the present day, when the feeling grows that "the times are waxing late," and the pre-millenarian's views are being expounded by so many men eminent for evangelical zeal and for sound scholarship. No one denies the fascination that there is in the blessed vision of the future that is unfolded by it; and every scholar knows the grave difficulties that stand in the way of its acceptance by many. But in all this the divine character is not involved. Our thought about God is not to be strained or changed by the position that we occupy in this matter. But our thought about God is involved in our conceptions of him as related to infant salvation, and the salvation of the heathen.

It may be said that faith should rise above gloomy doubts and fears, and should enable us with patience and confidence to wait for the revealing of the everlasting right. But it does not. The supreme desire of every pure soul is to know God. "Blessed are the pure in heart, for they shall see God." It is true that the finite can have but a partial vision of the infinite. We wait for the blessed time coming, when we shall know and shall see him as he is;

but, meanwhile, my vision of God must be real so far as it goes. I may see as in a glass darkly, but I cannot afford to have a distorted image. My conception of God, as far as it goes, must be satisfactory to my reason.

There is another class of moral and spiritual problems in which the character of God is involved. Take, for example, the allied questions of persecution and cruelty. Putting to one side the horrors of heathenism, let us consider the torture, cruelty, and oppression of the Christian era. The Spanish Inquisition has the bad pre-eminence of being the most notorious instance of heartless cruelty under show of law; but it was everywhere. Torture to extract confession was employed by the authorities in the case of political and civil criminals, as well as against heretics. The Tower of London and the Bastile of Paris had their dreadful stories of suffering just as the Spanish Inquisition had. Roman Catholics employed torture, and so did Protestants. Freedom of conscience was not understood. It was natural that the age that burned and drowned old women on charges of witchcraft should inflict the death penalty for comparatively minor offences against property. These atrocities were often perpetrated not only with the sanction of civil law, but also with the alleged authority of the Scriptures. It must be confessed that an age that dwelt more in the Old Testament spirit and times than in the sunlight of Christ, the Light of the World, could easily drift into the practising of such a sanguinary and gloomy criminal code. But, however much our Christian consciousness may be dismayed and shocked as we look back, however much some of the purer spirits who lived in those ages of cruelty might have been morally dismayed at the deeds which they witnessed, let us remember that the character of God is not at stake. We see all around us, now as well as then, the glaring injustices of the present, — the prosperity of the wicked, and the misery of those who are more sinned against than sinning; but we take refuge in that future in which right and truth will be vindicated, and sorrows will be healed, and tears will be dried. It is another problem when we have to think of children and of the heathen, for their doom is carried into that future which puts these other wrongs right. It is not only carried into the future, it is carried into an endless future.

While the sterner and gloomier view of revelation was the interpretation of the majority of the theologians of the seventeenth century, it cannot be asserted that the larger hope was without its advocates at all times. In "Eudoxa," by John Robinson, doctor of physics, published in 1658, when the author was an old man, he speaks of "The universal church out of which there is no salvation: And of this universal church many have been and are amongst the pagans, Turks, and remotest heretics saved by a way unknown to us: as little children are said to believe: Matt. xviii. 6." In the same treatise, and consistently with his own position, he gives a definition of justification which will be new to some even at the end of the nineteenth century. "Justification does not, as some will urge, always presuppose guilt; it sometimes may be a declaration of innocence." John Dove, who published a book in 1620, in which he criticises some of the views of John Robinson of Leyden, expresses his belief in the salvation of infants, and boldly affirms that the doctrine of original sin is an invention of Rome. He also declares that God reprobates none except those who reject his grace offered in his Son.

We take the theology of the century following the Reformation as our starting-point. We find two lines of thought concerning the fate of infants and of the heathen. The extreme Calvinism which was approved of by the great majority is the more logical of the two views. The amelioration of this view that has come into the heart of Christendom is not the result of new data, or of keener logic, or of more learned interpretation of Scripture. It is the result of the larger view of the character of God revealed in and to us by the Christian consciousness. The change in the hearts and thoughts of men as to the salvation of the little children has come to the front by a vigorous beating against the stream. Systematic theology was and is against it. The doctrines held by the churches of the Reformation were against it, while their opposition took different shapes. The guilt of Adam's first sin was a millstone round the neck of many trembling ones. The popular literature clothed the gloomy shadows with an unsparing realism. The change has come not from a change of creed, for creeds have been changed but little; not from a more learned exegesis, for the theology of the Reformation is exegetically strong; not from the positive teaching from the pulpit, for so far the pulpit is in the first stage of inevitable doctrinal change, — it is silent concerning the old, and also concerning the new; it has come from the apprehension and comprehension of the character of God[1] by the Christian consciousness. The fate of the heathen is to-day in the position which infant salvation held in the Christian consciousness fifty years ago. It does not necessarily follow that the universal salvation of the heathen will be accepted by the Christian consciousness.

[1] It is interesting to note that the age which evolved the Puritan and hyper Calvinistic conception of the character of God, also elaborated Milton's Satan. Considered as a literary conception, Satan is Milton's grandest character. "He has given the Devil his due," and more than his due; and the popular conception of the arch enemy of man is a compound of the devil of the miracle play, the Satan of Milton, and the Satan of Scripture. The first half of the seventeenth century could not do justice to the dignity of man. His Adam is commonplace.

CHAPTER X

THE CHRISTIAN CONSCIOUSNESS AND WOMAN'S PLACE IN THE CHURCH

MANY considerations unite to give much interest to the study of the relation of the Christian consciousness to the place and functions given to woman in the Christian church. It is a doctrinal question, but it is not a cardinal doctrine. So much is this the case that we exhibit a tendency to lose sight of it as a doctrine, and regard it as being a question of policy, or even of expediency. The line of cleavage in opinion as to the question does not separate denominations as such, but it has more or less significance in all denominations. This whole question has also been broadened by the advance on the part of woman being all along the line of life. In politics, in moral and social reforms, as well as in the church, she occupies a larger field than ever before. While the Christian consciousness has to do with her place in society, it is nevertheless true that this is primarily and principally a sociological and ethical problem. But when we discuss the place given to women in the past, and won by women in the present, in church life and work, we are on distinctively Christian territory; and the question becomes at once doctrinal, moral, and ethical. It is in the province of the Christian consciousness. From what has been said in some of the preceding chapters of this book, it will be evident that, no matter what the personal opinion of the author on this question may be, in the study of it as related to the Christian consciousness our object is not to support or to attack this movement for the emancipation of the sex, commonly called the weaker. Nor is it necessary that we should critically examine the argument from Scripture. But, on the other hand, I have no hesitation in the expression of my personal belief and conviction that, so far as the logic of the matter is concerned, the Presbyterian Church of the United States was consistently right in taking to task a prominent divine, still living, for admitting a woman into his pulpit. This matter is not new. It has always been in the church. The teaching of Paul is explicit and definite. There was an exception to his rule which he himself tacitly recognizes, and which the church has always been, on sufficient evidence, ready to recognize. This exception is the recognition of the divine afflatus and inspiration[1] descending upon a woman, and thus giving her a commission which set aside all earthly rules; but this was made the exception which proved the rule. Miriam, Deborah, and Anna in sacred story, and possibly some names in profane history, might be added as illustrating the prophetic utterance. But the Pauline *dictum* was the rule.

Macaulay, in his review of Von Ranke's "History of the Popes," draws attention, with all his usual eloquence, to the wisdom of Rome in providing moral and spiritual safety-valves for devout and enthusiastic women. Like all the rest of the world, she knew that woman's place was in the home, where she could influence for good the coarser nature of the husband, and train her children to be good Christians and good citizens; but there were many women who were practically homeless. They had neither husband nor children. And there were others

---

[1] Joel ii. 28, 29.

whose hearts were buried in the graves of their beloved dead, and in their souls they shrank from the possibility of another earthly love like this buried love. And there were still others who were stirred with other ambitions and other longings, and home life and home duties of the ordinary routine could not hold them. Rome, in her wisdom, made provision for such cases. The cloistered nun could shut out the world of which she was a-weary, and in prayer and vigil pass her days, or with nimble fingers and deft skill she sewed altar cloths and priestly vestments. The teaching nun could devote herself to a life that was at once religious and practical, while the Sisters of Mercy were the trained nurses of the past. To be sure, the church blundered occasionally, and women blundered occasionally.

It would have been better for Jeanne d'Arc if she had remained quietly with her few sheep in the wilderness, but it would not have been as well for France. The fifteenth century burns her as a heretic, and the nineteenth canonizes her. But it was simply impossible for the Maid of Orleans to stay at home. Abraham had to move at the Divine Voice. The magi must follow the star, and Jeanne had to run on God's errand. When women in the bosom of Protestantism felt this tugging at their heart-strings, for over two centuries, they had to sit still in the bitterness of defeat, or they had to risk their social standing and fair fame.

Robinson of Leyden, of Pilgrim Father fame, was, for his time, a liberal and fair-minded man. His testimony is significant. The church in London had written to Robinson and to his church about several things; among the others, this question as to woman's place in the church. His reply is dated at Leyden, fifth April, 1624. To their specific question "whether women have voices with men in the judgment of the church," he replies: "The apostle teacheth plainly the contrary (Cor. xiv. 34; 1 Tim. ii. 14); and though he speaks particularlie of prophesying and teaching, yet layes he down a more general rule, forbidding all such speaking as in which authority is used, that is usurped over the man, which is done speciallie in judgments. And if a woman may not so much as move a question in the church for her instruction, how much less may she give a voice, or utter reproof for censure." In another work,

"The People's Plea," he grants that she may teach outside the church, as the woman of Samaria did. The prohibition as regards women is in his opinion perpetual.

The history of the emancipation of woman has yet to be written; and when it finds a worthy historian, the world will have an opportunity of studying a social, moral, and doctrinal evolution of a very instructive character. Ordinary school teaching was almost entirely in the hands of men, not only in mixed schools, but also in those devoted to the education of girls. The dames' school for little children was tolerated. That the wife of the teacher in the higher class school should assist her husband was tolerated, just as the storekeeper's or shopkeeper's wife could assist her husband, or the daughter her father, long before they had advanced to the freedom of hiring female assistants. The invasion of the common or district schools of New England by women was an unheralded and noiseless revolution; and more and more of the work of teaching both sexes is being done by women. The opening of other avenues of usefulness was a question of time, and time was on their side; but their champions of their own and of the other sex had their work cut out for them by an unsparing criticism, which, when other argument failed, could always fall back, and very frequently did fall back, upon that moral and social scarecrow which was called an unsexed woman. But woman won her way; and it is only due to her place in this great social evolution to testify to the dignity and purity of the great leaders. It is natural and to be expected that any propaganda of this kind will draw to it the erratic, and those whose zeal outruns their discretion; but there has been less extravagance, less "bad form," as the world puts it, in this movement than in the total abstinence crusade, or in the abolition movement.

The church helped on the work by laying all unconsciously certain broad and deep foundations. Sunday-schools must be taught; and there was too often a dearth of men, and an abundance of willing female teachers; and so they took a prominent place in the Sunday-school. Missionaries had wives; and these good women not only helped their husbands, but they wrote home sad stories of their heathen sisters' ignorance, and of the almost impossibility of the missionary being able to approach them.

Sex was an impossible barrier to this zenana or harem life. Then, why not send out women missionaries, who could mingle with their sister women, and teach to them and preach to them the story of the Cross? They were sent; and after a few years' service they came back on furlough, and told to delighted audiences of women their story of work done; and ere long they addressed mixed audiences, and were even invited to occupy the pulpits on Sunday to give information concerning their work. To form women's missionary societies at home, with their own managers, secretaries, and treasurers, was an easy and natural step; for should they not work for and correspond with their sisters who were at the front in this holy war? It was only one step more for women to study medicine, whether to practise at home or to be medical missionaries in India. If any one imagines that all these developments came about easily and naturally, they have only to read the current religious newspapers of those times to know that every inch of the ground was gained very quietly, but in the face of opposition.

It was not in the nature of woman to make this a selfish fight. She sought her own rights, her own enfranchisement, and she is seeking them now, in so far as they are not yet secured; but the organized action of woman in favor of social purity and of Christian temperance gives them a prominent place among the social reformers of the day.

But perhaps the most far-reaching and significant movement affecting woman's place in the church is yet in its infancy. The Young People's Society of Christian Endeavor has been heartily accepted and adopted by the various denominations; and even those denominations that have not seen fit to join this army, and march under its banner, have paid it the sincere homage of imitation, and have banded their young people together on almost similar lines of constitution and of work. Now, this organization recognizes the absolute equality of the sexes in taking part in speaking and in praying, in holding office, and in conducting their services. In passing, attention may be called to the fact, that a similar condition of affairs exists in the Salvation Army. Is it not reasonable and to be expected that the lessons learned in the ranks of the Christian Endeavor Society will be, ere long, carried forward into the other departments of church life and work? Only a few years ago, and the doors of all our great universities were closed to women. Co-education and university training are now, to a large extent, within the reach of women in England and America. If some ambitious and devout Salvation lass, or Christian Endeavor young woman, should knock at the doors of our great theological schools, where, in wisdom, in fairness, or by all analogy, can the line be drawn? and when intellectually and spiritually equipped for the work of the ministry, what then? The ranks of law and medicine have been successfully invaded, and why should not the ranks of the preachers also open and welcome the elect and consecrated woman? You quote St. Paul. Of course he would be quoted and interpreted, and church history would be searched, as it has been, and the deliverances of synods and conferences and assemblies would be quoted; but the jewel of consistency has been thrown away by the church. If her exegesis of St. Paul is correct, she has conceded far too much already. In fact, the church in Britain and in America is responsible for the advanced stage of this question about the rights of woman, even if there is not a disposition to take the credit of the work. This beginning with the church is a hopeful sign, a veritable token for good in this cause. The order in which a revolution evolves indicates, and in a sense determines, its character. The French Revolution was first social, then political, and thirdly religious. The English Revolution was first religious, second social, and third political. The French Revolution produced Revolution number two in 1848, and the miserable beginning and ending of Louis Napoleon. The English Revolution produced the Reform Bill and the Victorian era. It is a sign for good, and a promise of success — this beginning of the emancipation of woman in the church.

While the whole question of woman's place in the life and work in the church, as well as in the political arena and in the social sphere, is still, as it were, on trial, it will be conceded by those who have given it earnest study and attention, that much has been gained, not because of current or past interpretation of Scripture, but against it. The Christian consciousness has thus far been on the side of this movement. It has given its sanction to the spirit of the age, and it has done its part in creating the spirit of the age. The popular phrase, "It is in the air," is accepted as explaining much; but while it is a very graphic description of a condition of things, it explains nothing. A correct science of physical or moral existence seeks after the efficient cause or causes of phenomena. Whence came this nebulous and partially defined thing that is in the air? Its existence, perhaps, can be accounted for. Social and moral evolution take us back very near to the origin, but they do not explain the genesis of it. Benjamin Kidd will tell us that it is not in the nature of man, the stronger, to part with any of his power or privilege to woman, the weaker; and that he does so only because of the ethical compulsion of the ultra-rational sanction which religion provides, and which causes this altruism. We can accept all this, with the addition that the altruistic sentiment has its origin in the Christian consciousness. Professor Drummond exalts the evolution of love, and in consistence with his philosophy will show how man rises by slow degrees to do justice to those whom he loves. We can accept this also, and add that the Christian consciousness opens the blind eyes of love, and enables it to see duty and justice.

A good many years ago George MacDonald said that it was not for man to say what woman should do and should not do. It was for women themselves to determine what was right and what was wrong. As we quote from memory, there is no approach to verbal accuracy in this reference; and, of course, there is the danger of even misstating the sentiment. He maintains that good women will find out what is their province. This suggests an interesting method of arriving at results. Suppose the question at issue were whether or not women should have every suffrage that man possesses in political life. They vote as to whether or not they want to vote. In such a case a majority of those who cast their votes would not be a satisfactory settlement, because it can readily be supposed that those opposed to voting would decline to vote, even on this general issue. But if a majority of the whole were to signify their desire to possess the suffrage, by what right, but that of the strongest, would man refuse to accede to their request. Should a case arise in the church, and the desire of women to exercise any function now denied to them, be clearly expressed, this wish of Christian women would be an expression of the results arrived at by their Christian consciousness. Suppose such an issue to come, and the result were to demonstrate that the Christian consciousness of men was opposed to the Christian consciousness of women. Who would decide? and to what final court of appeal could the conflicting parties go? An old-fashioned proverb speaks of the folly of jumping the fence before we come to it. Such a case has not yet emerged.

Many advocates of women's rights in the church and in the state would not be prepared to accept some of the positions indicated. With a good show of reason they would argue that, though the majority of women were not in favor of women practising law or medicine, or of voting for political offices, that is not sufficient reason for those who wished to do so having the privilege or right taken from them. They might say that it is not a question of majorities, but a question of inalienable right. But the inalienable right t has not the sanction and permission of the majority is not in the field of practical life. The right that is enjoyed by suffrance, whether it be the right of the early Christians to meet for worship with the shadow of paganism on them, or the right of the women of the nineteenth century to vote for members of Congress, may be enjoyed, and may be a source of gratification; but it only emphasizes the capricious tyranny that bestows it. There is no ultimate social or ethical good in it. WOMEN'S RIGHTS is, after all, the correct term. In the region of the spiritual, the Christian consciousness discerns rights and demands rights. Privileges can take care of themselves. A half-loaf is often better than no bread, but the right that is conferred as a privilege is a kind of moral insult.

The reader of "Gesta Christi," by Charles Loring Brace, will find a very interesting chapter on "The Position of Woman under Modern Influences;" and, although the author of that interesting work does not draw special attention to the fact, it is nevertheless obvious that every step in advance that has been gained by woman towards the Christian idea of her perfect equality with man in rights and in responsibilities has been secured grudgingly and unwillingly from man. The Christian consciousness which secured the ultra-rational altruistic sentiment was a moral compulsion before which the triple walls of strength, selfishness, and custom had to fall.

It is often claimed that there are two remarkable exceptions to this general rule, — in the case of woman in religious communities, and woman in the age of chivalry. I think the exceptions are more imaginary than real. In the seclusion of the religious community, there was self-government subject to the supremacy of the ecclesiastical authorities of the other sex. The outer world for centuries honored them for the sake of their work and life. They let the world alone; and the world let them alone, except when their broad acres and fair possessions stirred the cupidity of some robber baron, until he braved the church and risked his soul for the sake of present possession.

The age of chivalry has around it the glamour of romance, and it has proved a veritable mine of wealth to all writers of the romantic school.

Even the sage historians seem at times to revel in it, and to regard it as an oasis in a dreary desert of superstition, violence, and bloodshed. And this not without reason; for so long as barons, knights, and squires exalted women, paying sometimes a fanciful, and sometimes a real reverence, as in a boy's game where it is hard to tell where make-believe ends and reality begins, the love was idealized that might easily have been brutalized; and the lower ranks of society, ever ready to copy from their social superiors, would learn something of courtesy.[1] "To chivalry woman is indebted in the Middle Ages for a position she had never before enjoyed in history, which gave her a charm almost unknown till then, and which spread over a society steeped in barbarism a grace and refinement that have come down to our day." But after all, chivalry made women the counters with which men played at a game called chivalry. The tournament and the lists were a combination of the modern duel and athletic sports, and the knight-errant was not always the hero that Sir Walter Scott delights to portray. He was too often a soldier of for-

[1] Gesta Christi, page 284.

tune, a skilled swordsman, who was to the Middle Ages what the gladiator was to the Roman, what the prize-ring and college football are to nineteenth century civilization.

The benefit that it was to woman was incidental and accidental. Chivalry refined manners, but it did not accelerate justice. There was no Christian consciousness in it. But to-day the Christian consciousness has done its work, and woman has a place, and exercises functions, in the most conservative ecclesiastical bodies, which would have been promptly refused her fifty years ago; and the refusal would have been, and actually was, based upon the interpretation of the Scriptures which bore upon her case. The old exegesis was sound. It is as good now as it was then. The silence of confessions, catechisms, books of discipline, and articles of religion, on this question — the comparative silence — is accounted for by the simple fact that the necessity for any strong declaration was not even dreamed of. The Christian consciousness has been at work, and changes have been possible that have not been sanctioned in any other way. The end is not yet. Meanwhile, it is interesting to note the effort being made by that class of interpreters who begin by opposing a new movement, and have scarcely finished their effort to show that it is unscriptural, when they awake to the fact that this intruder has come to stay. Then it is in order to reconstruct their interpretation of Scripture on the question; and if the hands would go backward on the world clock, they, too, could fall back on their former exegesis.

CHAPTER XI

THE CHRISTIAN CONSCIOUSNESS AND THE SIXTH COMMANDMENT

Man has been defined as a fighting animal; and the most perplexing problem in moral and social evolution as well as in the function of the Christian consciousness, is presented to us by his readiness, in sport or in earnest, for pecuniary gain or for reputation, in proof of innocence or in desire for revenge, to fight with and to kill some other man. The thirst for blood, for exhibitions of physical and mental horrors in the arena, went hand in hand in Rome with the enjoyment of undisguised sensuality and indecency. Christianity waged war against this spirit and practice of the age; but the evil that appeals, not only to the baser passions of man, but also to sentiments that are akin to virtue, dies hard. Why should we express any surprise at its taking the church so long to suppress the bloody scenes of the amphitheatre in Rome and in the great provincial cities? It was an evil inheritance which had come down through centuries of heathenism. The Decalogue thundered, "Thou shalt not kill;" and Jesus gave the positive command, "Therefore, all things whatsoever ye would that men should do to you, do ye even so to them;"[1] but the red stream of innocent blood has ever been flowing. It began at the gates of Eden, and flowed on and on, a river of death, until the blood shed at Calvary fell into it; and the river is still flowing, and greedily drinking up the blood of the many murdered for robbery's sake, or in the duel, or in the sport that wantonly and uselessly risks man's life, or in that game of war which makes Europe a vast camp of armed men.

In Christian Europe, every Christmas morning comes with its story of the Prince of peace; and its joy-bells ring in the ears of five million Christians of a real or nominal kind, who are armed and willing, sometimes anxious, to fly at each other's throats. The poet says that, "Were the people wiser, war is a game kings would not play at;" but the pity of it is that the people seem to be as fond of it as are the kings.

[1] Matt. vii. 12.

The United States, removed from the arena of European conflict and interests, with a continent so great in extent and in variety of climate and of natural products that there was no need of war for enlarging her territory, seemed to be the one nation that could dispense with a vast standing army and have no dread of war; and yet perhaps the most religious and the most intelligent nation on the face of the earth, so far as the general diffusion of knowledge is concerned, drifts into a war, an internecine war, of unparalleled dimensions. After the hot carnage of four years, peace came from the exhaustion of one of the combatants; and the nation resumes its interrupted life, and with the real cause of the strife, slavery, abolished. A marvellous spectacle truly; but more wonderful still is the fact that thirty years after the strife is over, both parties profess to glory in the part that they or their fathers took, and the divisions among the followers of the Prince of peace which had their origin in this Cain and Abel fight are in existence still. This is a moral and religious problem which might be studied more earnestly with advantage to the cause of religion.

"Peace on earth" was the song of the host at the Annunciation. While we do not minimize the good that has been accomplished, the peace that has been promoted between factions and nations by the genius of Christianity, — the strifes that have been healed have been many, and peace that passeth understanding has come to longing souls in every age, — yet, in its larger outlook, Christianity has been more of a failure in this thing of which the angels sang than in any other department of morals. So much is this the case, so obviously is it true, that many writers on morals and on social and political economy have tried to prove that war is unavoidable, is necessary, is profitable to civilization as a whole. They hold that it is quite proper that the Christian should add to his good fight of faith against spiritual foes, a good deal of readiness for war in general. To prove that an overruling Providence sometimes brings good out of war, as he does out of other forms of evil, is simply a demonstration of the happy truth that he can make the wrath of man to praise him. The greater contains the less. If it is right for Germany and France to go to war to settle a difficulty, why should it be wrong for the individual Frenchman and German to settle their personal dispute by war which may take the shape of assassination or of the duel, and yet resemble national warfare? We are told that these belligerent individuals are inexcusable because they have legal redress, and at once can have recourse to it. But this assurance at once causes one to wonder how it comes to pass that nineteen centuries of Christianity have not devised a court of arbitration to which nations could resort, and the decisions of which could be enforced.

The church of history has in a feeble and half-hearted manner been on the side of peace. There has always existed a certain amount of Christian consciousness in favor of peace, but it took a long time for it to find expression in the " Peace Society." And when the society was at last evolved, it was in advance of the age, as witness the ridicule which was heaped upon its efforts by a large part of the public press. It concerned no dogma which divided sects, unless, indeed, we ought to give due credit to all the sects of the quietists who conscientiously refuse to fight. It did not come to the hearts and homes of men as slavery or intemperance did. The young hero going to the wars, and the old veteran covered with medals, scars, and glory, were both good to look upon. War was linked to patriotism and personal courage, and these are words to conjure with. When one man kills another for an acre of ground in dispute between them, the sooner the hangman is called in the better for society; but when opposing armies of a hundred thousand men decimate each other's ranks about some trivial territory or debatable point of honor, call it glory, burn bonfires, ring joy-bells, reward the survivors, praise the dead heroes, and make ready for another fight. Meanwhile, let us sing and preach and pray about the Prince of peace, for we are Christian nations.

Not only was there little or no Christian consciousness in favor of enforcing the sixth command of the Decalogue, it was almost altogether ignored. The death penalty was inflicted for comparatively trifling offences against property; and when the laws which made so little of human life were gradually taken from the statute-book, it was the severity of the punishment more than any consideration of the inherent dignity and value of life as life, which led to the amelioration.

The judicial combat was on the crude supposition that the divine judgment would be indicated by the result of the duel between the parties. If this appeal had taken the form of drawing lots as to which of the combatants should commit suicide, there would have been lottery in it. Napoleon is said to have remarked that Providence usually seemed to be on the side of the heaviest artillery; and in an age when physical strength had so much to do with the result of the fight, the absurdity of this form of settlement of personal feud must have been painfully apparent. It was a corruption of the old practice of the avenger of blood; and the church, with her rights of asylum and sanctuary, was to the feudal times what the city of refuge was to the Israelite in the time of the Judges. The judicial duel spread through Europe; and the church spoke against it for two hundred years before we find any civil enactment against it. The judicial duel did not altogether disappear until the seventeenth century. In fact, the wager of battle in certain cases came down to the beginning of the present century; and it was not legally abolished in England until 1819. The case in which it was so long permitted was the right to challenge any one acquitted of murder to the ordeal of single combat, the challenger being a relative of the murdered person.

The duel, the so-called field of honor, survives in all Christian countries, and only in some of them is it illegal. It has been said of it, "That there is no foolish thing so wicked, and no wicked thing so foolish." When the results are notoriously harmless, as in certain encounters in France, all the world laughs. When good men are killed by less worthy foes, all the world cries shame, and declares that the duelist is only a remove from the assassin. But the practice continues, and personal honor is the plea and excuse and justification. The prize-ring in England was quite as dangerous an institution as was the duel in France and Germany. British and American college boys run more risk of personal injury in the football field than do the much padded and carefully protected members of the fighting corps of certain German universities. Pugilism dies hard in English schools and in English and American athletics. The spice of danger, whether in riding after fox-hounds or in hunting tigers, is the exciting and pleasurable element in the sport. In providing amusement for the public, every showman knows that the feat that attracts is one in which the performer not only shows skill, but runs the risk of breaking his neck. We all like to sup on horrors of some kind or other. Let us confess it: we are a fighting race. The blood of warlike Normans and pirate Danes and stubborn Saxons and fiery Celts is in our veins; and in our secret souls cowardice is worse than minor crime. The thoughtless infliction of cruelty, and the stoical enduring of it when it comes to ourselves, is in the nature of us.

In the case of slavery and intemperance (in morals), and also in the case of the salvation of infants and of the heathen (in doctrine), we drew attention to the fact that the Christian consciousness asserted its sway, and brought positive convictions and moral certainty, where from the standpoint of biblical exegesis and criticism there was room for diversity of opinion. But here we have a positive commandment, one of the ten, habitually disregarded both in its letter and in its spirit. I knew a small boy who was, when at school, quite ready and willing to gratify the desire of the older pupils to get up a fight. When that boy went home bearing marks of the fray, if he had been beaten by a lad of his own age, or if he had suffered defeat at the hands of a smaller boy, he was usually soundly punished by an indignant parent for his misconduct, and for his quarrelsome disposition. But there were occasions on which he was a much disfigured boy with only one thing to console him, namely, he had succeeded in thrashing a bigger boy than himself in a more or less artistic fashion, and on these occasions the boy was gravely scolded, but not whipped, at home; and he came to know that the following day was the best time to make an appeal to his father for pocket-money. The pugnacity of the race, its inborn admiration of courage and endurance, retarded the development of the Christian consciousness. The merciful provisions of the Mosaic statute-book with regard to the lower animals did not produce societies for the prevention of cruelty to animals until the modern period. The modern pugilist on the stage will draw, not the same audience, but as large an audience, as a Patti or a Booth; and it apparently pays some clubs to pay many thousand dollars to two professional pugilists and rivals for the championship to settle the matter under their auspices and within their doors.

All healthy men and boys, and also all healthy women and girls, delight in stories of personal daring and endurance. Realism holds up a picture of life, and we say it is artistic. Idealism pictures life as it ought to be, or as it might be, and we say it is suggestive or charming. Romanticism pictures life in its heroic possibilities and impossibilities, and we say it is glorious. Revelation is realistic. No modern realist can improve upon the sententious brevity with which the good and evil of Noah, Abraham, Jacob, David, and others are related. It is idealistic, for running through the Word is the silver thread of a life that ought to be; and it is romantic, for its heroes and martyrs can thrill the soul. We cannot eradicate the admiration for strength and beauty, for they find a place in the presence chamber of God. Woe to the nation in whose schools and colleges athletic sports find no place, and whose people do not delight in manly sports! But the delight must consist in participating in them, not in merely looking on as spectators. When Greece and Rome were in their glory, their youth contended in the games. When they were in their corrupt decadence, they looked on while slaves fought with each other or with wild beasts for their amusement. The curse of professionalism is on the manly sports of our day; and professionalism says to the average citizen, "Pay your gate-money, and look on and applaud, and make your bets, and leave the athletics to our hired professionals." It may appear strange that popular amusements and the relation of the Christian consciousness to them should be related to the sixth commandment; but if the supreme attraction is the element of danger, and the skill which avoids the danger, the connection is at once apparent.

The whole question of the relation of the Christian consciousness to pain and suffering and death of man and the lower animals is in the crudest possible shape. Is there, or is there not, any connection between cruelty to others and indifference to danger in ourselves? Does the practice of torturing others make man more stoical in the enduring of physical pain? Let us suppose that the Christian ideal of the more advanced Christian consciousness were to become the rule of life. Nations have really beaten their swords into ploughshares, and their spears into pruning-hooks; "they learn the art of war no more." It is not the Millennium, and we have still a vigorous and effective police; but there is not a standing army within the borders of Christendom. The duel has become a thing of the past. Manly sports are cultivated, and the gymnasiums of colleges, Young men's Christian Associations, and other organizations, are well patronized; but a vigorous and successful effort has been made to so regulate exhibitions and games that the risk to life and limb has been reduced to a minimum. Professionalism has been regulated as far as law can; and the legislation against gambling, pool-selling, and betting has been so rigidly enforced that the amusements, if there were any, that could not exist without gambling, have disappeared. This is no impossible Utopia. It is a condition of things which we can imagine to exist twenty-five years hence, and to have been brought about without any moral or social convulsion. What would be the result upon the character of man? Would there be a loss in manliness and in courage? This has been boldly asserted by many writers. But it is difficult to find any reason for such conjecture. The increased estimate of the sacredness of human life would lift to a higher popular estimate the daring of our fire brigades and our life-boat service. A venerable Irishman of my acquaintance was in his youth so impressed with the dangers of coal-mining in the North of England, that with a due and prudent regard for his own personal comfort and safety, he enlisted in the British army, went through the whole of the Crimean war, and came out of it a sergeant with medals for distinguished service; and when he revisited the scenes of his youth, and heard of the accidents of various kinds, and witnessed the havoc that had been made in the ranks of his former associates, he came to the conclusion that his decision had been wise on the mere grounds of personal safety, even though he had fought in the Crimea and in the Indian mutiny. Peace has her battles, her victories, and her heroes, as well as war.

In the closing chapter of his "History of Humane Progress," C. Loring Brace expresses his belief that his history shows the existence of "A moral FORCE producing certain definite though small results during a certain period of time, and of a nature adapted to produce indefinite similar results in unlimited time."[1] He very justly claims that the granting of these premises proves Christianity to be the ultimate system of morals. His "moral force" is neither more nor less than the Christian consciousness; or granting that this power — not ourselves — outside of ourselves — which makes for righteousness — the moral force, being not ourselves, and outside ourselves, is not and cannot be Christian consciousness. Such a power is supernatural and ultra-rational, and it can find its expression only in the Christian consciousness. Philosophy provides the mechanism, and religion provides the motive-power, for all moral progress. The Christian consciousness discerns and applies the motive-power. Why was there so little development in morals

[1] Page 469.

until the Reformation? There was no lack of philosophy; but it was neglected for scholasticism, and there was no motive-power in the church. It is one of the great enigmas of the history of mind and morals, that Plato's "Republic" should have had so little influence upon the social, moral, and ethical life of the world. For two thousand years the world had this masterpiece, and not till these two millenniums had come and gone, did its lofty thought begin to blend with Christian culture in bettering the life of man.

I may be permitted to remind the reader of the main contention and design of this chapter. In our previous instances and illustrations of the relation of the Christian consciousness to evolution in morals and in doctrine, I have endeavored to show that the Christian consciousness, in its apprehension of God and in its conception of his character, led the way, or gave its sanction, to evolution and development in morals and in doctrine which sometimes seemed to antagonize our creeds and disregard our exegesis. But in this chapter we have considered certain phases of life, all bearing on the letter or on the spirit of the sixth command of the Decalogue, in which the Christian consciousness not only seems to be at times inoperative, but at other times seems to retard the church in her pronouncements against certain moral and social evils. That the Christian consciousness should play such a part does not interfere with our acceptance of the belief in its existence and in its activity. It enables us to hail the signs of its awakening in the directions indicated as the dawn of a better day in the life of the world.

CHAPTER XII

OBJECTIONS AND POSSIBILITIES

EVOLUTION or development in morals is denied by some who are recognized champions of orthodoxy, as that word is used from the Protestant point of view. This has been made easy by its natural opposition to the ethical and moral systems which profess to improve upon and to supplant the Christian system. Since these non-Christian systems all hold to the evolution of morals, is not the contrary true of Christian morality? To many minds, evolution in morals appears to be a playing fast and loose with the everlasting right and wrong. It is rhetorically convincing to assert that right can never become wrong. That is true so far as it is said regarding God's estimate of things; but, as a matter of fact, history tells us that so far as men are concerned, the thing that was right two hundred years ago is wrong to-day. To this it may be replied that slavery, drinking customs, and certain harsher dogmas, were wrong then, as they are now, but that men did not know any better. It is man's thought that changes, not God's thought. God's supreme wisdom is not in question. Moral philosophy is the science of human conduct, not of the divine administration. So far as man is concerned, evolution is as true in moral as it is in social and in physical life; and evolution in morals implies evolution in doctrine, for life of the consistent self-respecting kind must always be the outcome of that which a man believes. The following quotation may be taken as fairly representing the school of thought to which we refer. It is a form of apologetic that one shrinks from attacking, because one feels either that he does not understand, or that he himself is not understood: —

"But moral laws — whatever has been our progress in the knowledge of mind, of human physiology, of climatic influences, of social reactions — have made no progress since they were laid down by the Author of Christianity. Human philosophies, many and able, have been propounded — new ones are still propounded — as substitutes for the ethics of Christianity;

and yet not one of its principles has been invalidated, not a new one has been added to them. The moral law was long ago completed; its statutes have been established forever. . . . What the combined ingenuity of man has thus been unable to improve, we may justly conclude the combined ingenuity of man was incapable of originating or of discovering. . . . The Almighty *made* no moral laws, but created man in his own image. The moral laws of the divine nature were incorporated in the nature of man."[1]

If our author means that no moral precept of Jesus has been proved to be wrong, or has had to be modified or reversed, all Christians, and almost all theists, will heartily agree with him. If he means that correct morals and ethics with regard to slavery, the use of stimulants, and the other developments in morals to which reference has been made in this work, were all wrapped up in the precepts and example of Christ, and only waited their unfolding, he will again find himself in harmony with Christian thinkers and with many theists.

[1] President E. G. Robinson, D.D., LL.D. Christ and Modern Thought. Boston, 1880-81.

If he is speaking of the Decalogue, neither more nor less, all are agreed. But he uses such expressions as "moral laws" and "the moral law" as being interchangeable, which is certainly a little confusing. When he affirms that the combined ingenuity of man has not been able either to originate or to improve moral law, we are in hearty accord with him; for the Christian consciousness is not to be identified with human ingenuity pure and simple, as we have tried to prove. When he says that the Almighty *made* no moral laws, but created man in his own image, — "The moral laws of the divine nature were incorporated in the nature of man," — we accept the statement as being a very graphic statement of that dignity of man which is the theme of the second chapter of this book. But we fail to find in these words any proof that there has not been an evolution in morals. He makes an assertion, and then proceeds to prove something else. It is not to be expected that Christian or even theist will accept an evolution in morals having its cause in the "combined ingenuity of man." In the evolutions or development of morals, there can be no reconciliation of science and religion by any philosophy or course of reasoning which ignores or denies the Christian consciousness. It was absolutely necessary that he should assert that moral laws had "made no progress since they were laid down by the Author of Christianity;" for if they had their origin in "the infinitely perfect nature of a supreme and archetypal being," how could change be possible? But it is easy to imagine, and also easy to prove, that God left man an undiscovered country in matter, intellect, and morals, to which he was to apply the powers with which God had endowed him, and in which he has made notable progress.

There is a meretricious kind of rhetoric, with which, however, we are far from associating the learned author whose opinions we have been considering, which takes a loud and long delight in assuring the public that the Lord's Prayer, the Ten Commandments, and the Sermon on the Mount can never cease to be the very voice of God to us struggling, sinning, repenting, and aspiring mortals. Of course they cannot. Even those agnostics and theists who refuse to entertain our doctrines concerning the inspiration of Scripture are ready to confess the surpassing excellence of these passages, and their singular adaption to the social and moral life of man. We all bow in lowliest reverence before Him who spake as never man spake. The Decalogue is the Magna Charta of the moral order of the world. But these three marvellous words do not tell us everything. We look in them in vain for the morals of slavery, of marriage, of the points of submission to and of resistance to civil and religious authority. The direct teaching of the Word of God is binding on every man, and he has to beware how he reads it. The inferential teaching, that comes to us in its spirit rather than in its letter, is also binding; and we have to beware how we reason about it. God holds us to a stern and strict accountability. Our consciences and his Word agree as to this. We are, in the midst of our ethical difficulties and moral perplexities, entitled to cry out, "Teach me thy law." We can heartily agree with Dr. Robinson when he affirms that "the moral laws of the divine nature were incorporated in the nature of man;" but with the same starting-point we reach an entirely different conclusion. The moral law of the divine nature, incorporated in the nature of almost all the Christian men and women of the South, led them to say with all honesty, "Domestic slavery is a Scriptural institution, and the Abolitionism of the North is atheistical;" and the same law led the Christian opponents of slavery to say that slavery was the sum of all villanies, and was in direct antagonism to the spirit of Christ. It is true that murder can never cease to be murder; but the question that changes is as to what kinds of killing we shall call murder. It is very well to say that moral laws have not been changed since they were laid down by the author of Christianity, and it would be high treason to our King to assert anything to the contrary. We do not say (who does say?) that any word of Christ's can pass away. Ethical systems, which ignore religion, have been attempted; but even their contention is not with the word or with the spirit of Christ, as they are at great pains to affirm; but it is with the moral systems that have been developed in the Christian era.

It is easy to affirm, and it is not difficult to believe, that every possible change for good will be found to be in harmony with the example and precepts of Jesus. We can imagine a state of society in which drunkenness was very rare, in which there were not many requiring charity, and when it was required, it was freely given, and received without loss of self-respect. We can imagine a good time to come, when social unrest and discontent will be extremely rare, and when the war and greed and violence which sometimes mark the relations of labor and capital shall have passed away. And we believe that it is only the spirit of Christ that can secure this. When it does come, those who are then living will say that the truth and mercy and justice, the altruism and the love, which then control the lives of men, were always in the teachings of Jesus; but men's ears were stopped so that they could not hear; and they had eyes, but they did not see. All this may be — we believe is — true ; but there is an evolution, both in morals and in doctrine. This is the simple fact of history. We may give it many names. One says it is the new light that is ever streaming from the Word of life. Another says it is the work of the energizing Spirit. It is line upon line, precept upon precept. We get truth as we are able to bear it. Development in morals as in doctrine does not imply that the original type or primal statement of the truth has been reversed or changed. Truth is a living thing. It is the word of life. Like every living thing, it must grow, change, and develop.

The thought of the finite creature is limited, it is not necessarily immortal; but the thought of the infinite One is unlimited and immortal. Nor does it live in the unchanging stereotype. A prophet of Israel assures us that God distinctly declares that his thoughts are unlike man's.[1] In what respect are they unlike? There is an infinite difference represented by the distance between heaven and earth. That is a difference of degree, but there is also a difference in kind. The rain and the snow come down, and make the earth fertile and life-sustaining. So it is with God's Word. It does not return to him void. It accomplishes that which he pleases. It never fails to reach the point to which it has been sent. This is the difference between the divine word and the human word. Our words may be meaningless, misleading, insincere, truthful, living, or life-

---

[1] Isa. lv. 8–10.

less. When God or man speaks a living word, it grows. Christ spake as never man spake, because they were living words, and they have been growing ever since with the bloom of immortality on them. The Word of God lives and abides forever; but it does not abide in an everlasting monotone. It grows because it lives. What Dr. Robinson means when he says, "But moral laws — whatever has been our progress in the knowledge of mind, of human physiology, of climatic influences, of social reactions — have made no progress since they were laid down by the Author of Christianity," is hard to determine.

In the opening lecture of the volume from which the quotation under consideration was taken, Joseph Cook says: "If we follow the mind of the Spirit, we shall utter to our age our secret convictions. If we follow the impulse of the finger of the Spirit upon our souls, as we are differently trained by God's providence and by this constant touch of Christ's pierced right hand, we shall utter messages so diversified as to meet the diversified wants of our age." Joseph Cook has himself been the proof of the correctness of the faith and hope which he expressed in these words fifteen years ago. It is easier to harmonize these eloquent words with the doctrine of the Christian consciousness and the evolution of morals, than to harmonize them with the views of Dr. Robinson.

Sir James Mackintosh anticipated some of the problems of to-day, when in his study of the "Progress of Ethical Philosophy" he said that the agreement as to the rule of life was plain. The question is as to how men have come to agree in the rule of life. He might have added that it was also an interesting study as to how men came to disagree in the rule of life. The agreement is on a few general principles, and on certain abstractions called virtues which men persist in defining for their own benefit. Moral science always asks the question: "What ought to be? what is right? what is truth?" She knows what the everlasting ought and right and truth are: and in the practical application of them she makes progress. What is the ought and right and truth about this man who denies the things that most men believe? Moral science in the sixteenth century replies: "The stake, the inquisition, or, if you will be merciful, fine, imprisonment, and banishment." Moral science to-day says: "Persuasion is lawful; coercion in every form is unlawful." The theologian of the seventeenth century said, as an exegete and as a moral philosopher, the Bible teaches the existence of witchcraft; it gives both example and precept as to the treatment of witches. Certain persons are charged with witchcraft here in our midst. They are tried, and the evidence is found satisfactory as a proof of guilt. What remains to be done? Why, only this — that we must honor by imitation the Bible method of treating witchcraft. The logic is faultless. It was the Christian consciousness which rebelled.

Much might be said about the presence or absence of the Christian consciousness in sectarianism. The great majority of men are in the religious denomination to which they belong by inheritance and by environment. While it can be granted that the great majority of each denomination are intelligently persuaded that theirs is the best, or as good as any, their conviction did not lead them into their particular fold, although it may help to keep them there. We grant the scholarship and honesty of the founders of Episcopacy, Presbyterianism, Congregationalism, Methodism, etc. But they cannot all be right. It may be that not one of them is right. We grant the honesty and the scholarship of the contemporary champions of these sects. But we cannot believe that the Spirit has led any sect into the truth, the whole truth, and nothing but the truth; although ardent apologists are ready to claim all this for each of them. When the Christian consciousness is developed, the oneness for which the Christ prayed will come. There is spiritual law in the natural world. We are, as denominations and as congregations, apart from each other, because we are apart from Christ our Life and our King. Were He to appear on some swelling mount in the midst of a vast prairie, and were the world gathered round to greet the King. All eyes are fixed upon the mount of vision. From north, south, east, and west they look up to this hill of God. When at last the vision of his beauty and his glory fills their eyes and their hearts, by the mighty power of love they are moved to take some steps nearer to the mount on which they behold the shining feet of the Son of God. By these steps towards a common centre, they are every man drawn nearer to every other man. The nearer we are to Christ, the nearer we must be to each other.

Grindelwald Conferences, Evangelical Alliances, and Committees on Union, appointed by different denominations, are all very good; but they are all empiric, except in so far as they help the development of that fulness of the Christian consciousness which will make separation as impossible as union now is. When we take comfort in saying that our failure to secure a consensus in dogma or in morals is parallel to our failure to secure agreement in science or in politics, we write our own condemnation, because we have a solvent of our difficulties which they do not possess.

Schleiermacher died in 1834. He became more evangelical towards the end of his life, and the whole tendency of his teaching was one of reconciliation. He believed that theology could be rescued from that degradation which was caused by its changing with the continually changing systems of philosophy. He magnified the inner life of the soul in its relation to God. With him religious feeling meant absolute dependence on God. He was against both supranaturalism and rationalism; but he believed in the possibility of their reconciliation. In his Christian ethics, the

Christian consciousness is his foundation and starting-point. He tried to reconcile science with religion. We do not wonder at the influence for good that his writings have had upon much of our modern religious thought. But it must be granted that so far as the Christian consciousness is concerned, his influence was against its favorable reception by the Christian world. Schleiermacher had all the strength and the weakness of the great German thinkers. His strength lay in his originality as a thinker, his profound reverence for God, and his efforts at reconciliation of opposing doctrines. His weakness was that of more than one great German theologian. He had to found a school and to construct a system. The Christian consciousness was a reality; but instead of patiently endeavoring to find the law of it in the individual and in the community, and the evidences of it in history, he puts it on a throne, and makes it supreme. He rejects the Trinity because it is not in the field of the Christian consciousness. No wonder that orthodoxy became alarmed, and imagined that this new thing was a cunning device of the enemy.

We find certain writers using it to maintain their position in eschatology, inspiration, and so forth; but a weapon must not be judged by the arm that wields it, or by the motive which causes the blow. As we have already stated in a preceding chapter, we make no claim for the infallibility of the Christian consciousness: but it is well to remember that to the individual the Christian consciousness is absolute certainty. To separate error of which we may feel very certain from that concerning which the Christian consciousness gives us certainty, is not always an easy task.

The scepticism that was based on the asserted antagonism of physical science to the teachings of the Scriptures has lost much of its importance, not only because theology has reconciled some of the statements of science with the teaching of Scripture, but also because science has been again and again proved to be crude and hasty in her conclusions. Some of the most eminent scientific men of our day are earnest Christians, and able defenders of revealed religion. It is easy to anticipate and to believe in that comparatively near future, when the last echoes of the controversy between science and religion shall have died away, and the conflict of the last fifty years shall have become a matter of historical rather than of living interest.

The higher criticism is for the most part reverent; and while its opponents call it *destructive*, it calls itself *constructive*. But even were its avowed purpose the assault on revealed religion which its opponents claim that it is, it is a controversy that has in itself the promise of finality. Were the conflict limited to textual criticism and analysis, the opinions of the opposing groups of scholars would, ere long, assume definite shape; and the questions at issue would be settled as the millennarian question is settled, or as the question as to the subjects and mode of baptism is settled, — that is, by the recognition of irreconcilable difference of interpretation which we may in charity and in self-complacence lay at the door of the constitution of the human mind. Whether this is the only possible settlement, is an open question. It is possible, but not probable, that advancing scholarship and archæological discoveries may give complete victory to one or other of the opposing critical schools. Resolutions as to original autographs are proofs of temper rather than of conviction; but resolutions prove nothing. When the thing to be believed is settled by a majority vote, the minority ought to be dealt with in no uncertain fashion. Meanwhile, notwithstanding the lack of wisdom which both parties have occasionally exhibited, we may rest assured that the worst of the storm has blown over, and that the churches of Britain and America are not to be rent asunder by the higher criticism.

The Christian consciousness has no place in the questions at issue between science and religion, or in the questions raised by the higher criticism, except in so far as ever the character of God may be involved; and many hold that the character of God is not involved in those issues. When the time of a correct historical perspective has been reached, and some scholar of the future shall bring the history of apologetics up to date, the conflict between science and religion and the years of the higher criticism will be but incidents and episodes of a mighty whole.

The moral difficulty is perennial and persistent. It has been the stronghold of scepticism of every shade throughout the centuries. We may put to one side all consideration of of dishonest doubt; the doubt that is to honest doubt what hypocrisy is to religion: the doubt that traffics on itself, and exhibits its sores for money; the doubt that makes itself the justification of an unclean life, or in any other way demonstrates that it is a conscious lie. Such a perversion of the moral nature has to be classed with other forms of open or of secret sin.

But there is honest doubt; and while we may not be able to agree with Tennyson when he said that there lived more faith in honest doubt than in half the creeds, our hearts go out in loving kindness to the men who beat their way from doubt to faith until at length the discord of their lives becomes divinest harmony. We can and do respect the men of clean lives, — men who are faithful to domestic ties and to public duties, — even when they, with apparent relish at their work, persistently assail revealed religion. Goethe somewhere remarks that the mark of an honest doubter is his desire to get rid of his doubts. We will not presume to judge men; and, therefore, we dare not say how many of our sceptical writers of to-day are honest according to this standard. The test is too severe, for we may concede honesty to the doubter who is not conscious of any desire to get rid of his doubts. But while granting this, we may well doubt the moral honesty of the sceptic who can live and die without earnest longing for the faith and the peace which he sees in others. Christian living and dying is not a theory or a dream. It is an every-day reality.

But there is honest doubt, and there are honest doubters. This doubt is moral, even when we call it intellectual. The intellect is called into the service of doubt, for honest doubt must ever seek to justify itself. The Christian consciousness of the believer enables him to touch this doubt with healing. God asks us to prove him and try him. He has made us in his image, and given us dignity. God judges us, and we must judge God. We must be able to know clearly what we think about God and Christ. We can only justify God to man in proportion to our consciousness of God. The mission of Christ was to reveal the Father; and the more of the Christian consciousness that we possess, the more shall we be able to reveal God to others. In its last analysis, honest doubt is not the questioning of miracles, or inspiration, or the immortality of the soul; it is a misapprehension of the nature and the character of God. Some Christians and many theists are worshipping an idol of their own making which they call God. "Show us the Father and it sufficeth us."[1] The Christian consciousness reveals God.

There are many earnest and diligent observers of the signs of the times who see in the close of our century the most momentous time in the history of the world. Many of those who do not dabble in figures and dates in search for that hour which no man knows, are, nevertheless, persuaded of the probability of the near approach of the end of the age. There are others whose reasoning does not lead them in this direction, who are convinced that we are on the eve of stupendous political, social, and religious changes. Some publicists are sufficiently daring to assert that another great European war is impossible; but that if

[1] John xiv. 8.

it does occur, it will lead to the swift overthrow of this overgrown militaryism, which, like a dead weight of barbarism, clings round the neck of Christian civilization. When the hour and the man come, the province of the Christian consciousness will be recognized as it has not been in the past.

The three greatest movements of the latter half of our closing century in religious life and work are Young Men's Christian Associations, the Salvation Army, and the Young People's Societies of Christian Endeavor. Sir George Williams, General Booth, and Dr. Clark, the justly esteemed fathers and founders of these three world-wide movements, are all at the front, each one being still at the head of the body which he founded. Each one of these great movements has risen by leaps and bounds from obscurity and comparative insignificance into the world fame which it now has. It may be safely asserted that none of these three great leaders saw the world-wide name and fame that were coming to the societies which they organized. While they are fit men, men of will power, and of administrative ability, as well as of personal consecration to their good work, none so ready and willing as they are to confess that they did not see the grand future, but they were conscious of present duty. Their Christian consciousness approved the thing that they did. The Young Men's Christian Association had to win its way against the lukewarmness, the suspicion, and even the active opposition, of ministers and of churches; but the movement had friends as well as opponents among the clergy. The Salvation Army was subjected to the rough and ready abuse of the mob, and to the petty tyranny of the Dogberries, who are not all dead. The majority of church-going, respectable people voted it a well-meant extravagance, and would have hailed its natural extinction with satisfaction, though they upheld their right to march army fashion. To-day the Salvation Army is one of the great factors in all social problems, and the self-willed and erratic ex-Methodist preacher is consulted by bishops and statesmen. Learning and culture join in applauding the old hero; but he has not forgotten the days when decayed cabbages and ancient eggs were thrown at him.

The Young People's Societies of Christian Endeavor made such a quick march into all the churches, and overcame all question and opposition so quickly, that we almost forget that there was any question or debate or opposition. God is in his world; and in his moral and spiritual world he is in it by being in the hearts of men. These three men were chosen for this work that was given to each of them. They could not perhaps quote chapter and verse for every step that they took; but it was a pathway of prayer, and their Christian consciousness was contented.

Our denominations and our common Christianity have achieved much. There is no need for pessimism; but the failures are many, and the strifes are many. When the hour and the man come that shall lead us into the better time that is coming, there may be antagonism, but the victory is sure. The Christian consciousness will save us from the selfishness that characterizes our administration of our material possessions, and from the strife and vainglory of ecclesiasticism. Its positive gift to the church of the future is that largeness of view which will enable the denominations to forget their dead past, and to go forward one army to possess the earth. The good time coming will in some things resemble the church before schisms rent her, and heresies distressed her. "One body, one spirit, one hope, one Lord, one faith, one baptism, one God and Father of all, who is above all, and through all, and IN YOU ALL."[1] "God in us" is the key to the whole. This is the fairest and fullest expression of the "Christian consciousness."

There have been developments in morals and in dogma that are ultra-biblical so far as all current and antecedent exegesis was concerned. After the evolution was an accomplished fact, an *ex post facto* interpretation comes to the front, and justifies the WAYS OF MAN TO GOD. It vaguely defines itself as the spirit, in contradistinction from the letter, of the word.[2] No passage has been of such various use as this in which Paul draws a sharp contrast between the method and genius of the Old and New Testaments. The doctrine of the Christian consciousness solves past difficulties, and promises a future of gracious possibilities. It is always reverent. It believes in the indwelling Christ. The dispensation of the Spirit can never thrill the world with holy purpose until the Christian

---

[1] Eph. iv. 4 6.   [2] 2 Cor. iii. 6.

consciousness is heartily recognized and accepted. The Christ in us struggles in vain for fullest expression until we hail the Christian consciousness. The Christian consciousness has ultra-biblical sanctions, but it has no ultra-Christian sanctions in morals and in dogma. "For other foundation can no man lay than this is laid, which is Jesus Christ."[1]

[1] 1 Cor. iii. 11.

www.ingramcontent.com/pod-product-compliance
Lightning Source LLC
Chambersburg PA
CBHW021400230426
43666CB00006B/595